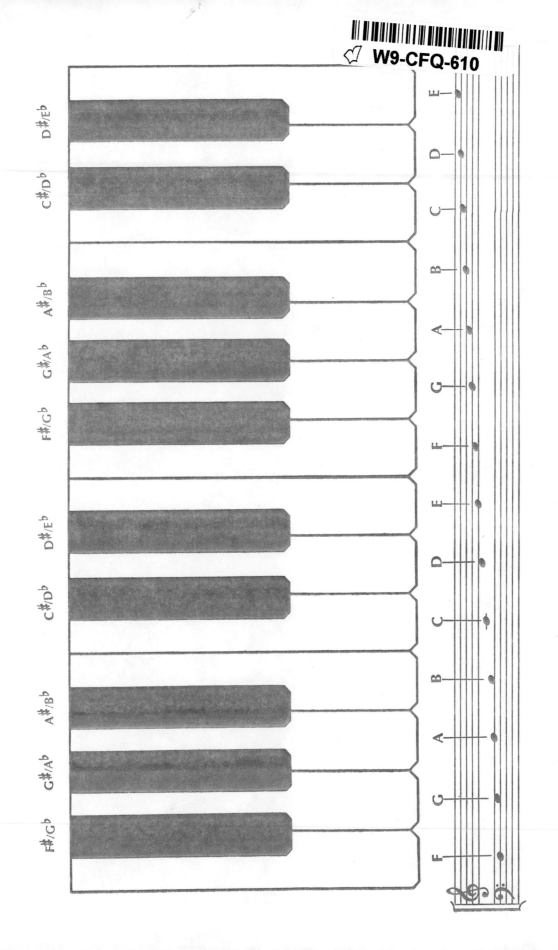

World of Music

JANE BEETHOVEN • JENNIFER DAVIDSON

CATHERINE NADON-GABRION

Authors

CARMINO RAVOSA

Theme Musical

JILL TRINKA

Reading Music

DARRELL BLEDSOE

Producer, Vocal Recordings

PHYLLIS WEIKART

Rhythmic Competency

Silver Burdett & Ginn

Morristown, NJ • Needham, MA

Atlanta, GA • Cincinnati, OH • Dallas, TX • Deerfield, IL • Menlo Park, CA

CONTENTS

SING ABOUT YOUR LAND

Woody Guthrie was a folk singer who made up hundreds of songs about America. This song is probably his best-known.

This Land Is Your Land

Words and Music by Woody Guthrie

I saw be-low me _____ that gold-en val-ley, _____

This land was made for you and me. _____

D.C. al Fine

2. I've roamed and rambled and I followed my footsteps
   To the sparkling sands of her diamond deserts,
   And all around me a voice was sounding,
   "This land was made for you and me." *Refrain*

3. When the sun comes shining and I was strolling
   And the wheatfields waving and the dust clouds rolling,
   As the fog was lifting a voice was chanting,
   "This land was made for you and me." *Refrain*

If you made up a song
about your land, what are
some of the things you might sing about?

PARTY IN THE BARN

When you shuck corn, you peel off the husks—the outside covering. Long ago, people harvested the corn by hand. Then as they shucked the corn, they shared stories and sang songs together. When they finished their work, they had a party.

Shuckin' of the Corn

Folk Song from Tennessee

1. I have a ship on the o - cean, _____
2. The wind blows cold in _____ Cai - ro, _____

All lined with sil - ver and gold. _____
The sun re - fus - es to shine. _____

Be - fore I'd see my true love suf - fer,
Be - fore I'd see my true love suf - fer,

That ship should be an - chored and sold. _____
I'd work all the sum - mer time. _____

REFRAIN

I'm a - go - ing to the shuck - in' of the corn, _____

Flora L. McDowell from MEMORY MELODIES

I'm a-go-ing to the shuck-in' of the corn, _____

A - shuck-in' of the corn and a-blow-ing of the horn,

I'm a - go-ing to the shuck-in' of the corn. _____

● Play a Pattern

Use sandblocks to play the **steady beat**. Tap the tambourine on the first beat of every **measure**.

Sandblocks

Tambourine

HUSKING BEE, ISLAND OF NANTUCKET, 1876   *Eastman Johnson*

DOWN ON THE FARM

Did you ever
hear of a goat
who ate a
rose?

This song tells about such a goat.
What other animals does the song
tell about?

Grandma's Farm

Words and Music by Cynthia Todd

1. I had a lit - tle goat on Grand - ma's farm,
2. I had a lit - tle goose on Grand - ma's farm,

And that lit - tle goat was mine.
And that lit - tle goose was mine.

She ate a rose and the gar - den hose
She bit the dog and the tail of the hog

© 1985 Cynthia Todd

8 **Songs about Farming**

And the sheets on Grand - ma's line.
And she hid be - hind the vine.

And the sheets on Grand - ma's line,
And she hid be - hind the vine,

And the sheets on Grand - ma's line,
And she hid be - hind the vine,

She ate a rose and the gar - den hose
She bit the dog and the tail of the hog

And the sheets on Grand - ma's line.
And she hid be - hind the vine.

3. I had a little pig on Grandma's farm,
   And that little pig was mine.
   She snorted once and snorted twice
   And she slept underneath the pine.
   And she slept underneath the pine,
   And she slept underneath the pine.
   She snorted once and snorted twice
   And she slept underneath the pine.

4. I had a little cow on Grandma's farm,
   And that little cow was mine.
   She ate all day and ran away,
   Said Grandma, "It's a crime."
   Said Grandma, "It's a crime."
   Said Grandma, "It's a crime."
   She ate all day and ran away,
   Said Grandma, "It's a crime."

A New Home Far Away

Many people who came to the United States from other countries came here to start a better life. Some farmers from Norway thought Oleana would be a good place to settle. Do you think they believed the words of this song?

Oleana

Norwegian Emigrant Song   English Words by Polly Budd

1. O - le-an - a, O - le - an - a, Far a - cross the deep blue sea,
REFRAIN: O - le, O - le - an - a, ___ O - le, O - le - an - a,

O - le - an - a, O - le - an - a, That is where I'd like to be.
O - le, O - le, O - le, O - le, O - le, O - le - an - a.

2. Oleana, that's the place,
   That is where I'll settle down;
   It's a place where land is free
   And money trees grow all around.

3. Corn and wheat grow to the sky,
   All according to the plan;
   Sheep and cows do all the work
   And fish jump in the frying pan.

4. There the crops just plant themselves,
   There the sun shines night and day;
   Harvest time comes once a month,
   But farmers only sing and play.

5. Ole Bull will play for us,
   Play upon his violin;
   And we'll sing and dance together,
   Happier than we've ever been.

Play a Pattern

Here are three patterns you can use to accompany
"Oleana." Team up with two friends and practice on
your own.

MOTHER CORN

It was the Native Americans who taught the early settlers how to raise corn.

Pawnee Indians spoke of corn as *Atira,* meaning "mother." *H* means "breath of life." This shows how important corn was in their lives. They sang this song to celebrate the harvest.

H'Atira

Pawnee Corn Song

Fol-low Moth-er Corn, Who breathes forth life.

H'A-ti-ra, H'A-ti-ra, H'A-ti-ra, A-ti-ra,

H'A-ti-ra, A-ti-ra, H'A-ti-ra, A-ti-ra,

A-ti-ra, H'A-ti-ra, A-ti-ra.

Drum and Rattle

Play the drum and rattle patterns as an **introduction.**
You can also use the patterns to accompany the song.

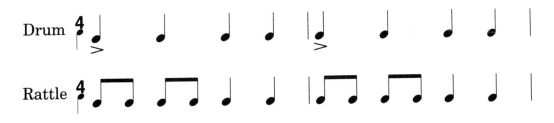

Far as Man Can See

Far as man can see,
  Comes the rain,
  Comes the rain with me.

From the Rain-Mount,
Rain-Mount far away,
  Comes the rain,
  Comes the rain with me.

O'er the corn,
O'er the corn, tall corn,
  Comes the rain,
  Comes the rain with me.

'Mid the lightnings,
'Mid the lightning zigzag,
'Mid the lightning flashing,
  Comes the rain,
  Comes the rain with me.

Far as man can see
  Comes the rain,
  Comes the rain with me.

From Song of the Rain-Chant

A Happy Song

People often sing and dance when they are happy.
This Navaho Indian song was sung at feasts and
on other joyous occasions.

When you sing the song, let your voice show
that the song is a happy song.

Navaho Happy Song

Navaho Indian Song

Hi yo, hi yo, ip si ni yah, hi yo,

Hi yo ip si ni — yah, hi — yo, Hi yo ip si

ni yah, hi — yo, Hi yo ip si ni yah,

(Last time only)

Ip si ni yah!

Courtesy of Janet Tobitt from THE DITTY BAG.

In this recording you will hear members of the
Navaho tribe singing one of their songs.

Navaho Night Chant . . . . . . American Indian

● Drum and Rattle Accompaniment

Here are two parts for instruments. Which part will
you play to accompany the singing?

I Walk with Beauty

In beauty happily I walk.
With beauty before me, I walk.
With beauty behind me, I walk.
With beauty below me, I walk.
With beauty above me, I walk.
With beauty all around me, I walk.

It is finished again in beauty,
It is finished in beauty,
It is finished in beauty,
It is finished in beauty.

From *The Night Chant, A Navaho Ceremony*

MAKING INSTRUMENTS

Native Americans accompany their songs and dances by playing instruments. You can make your own instruments and play accompaniments for songs in your book.

● Drums

A long time ago, people in certain tribes made a drum by turning a basket upside down on the ground. They would beat the drum with a stick. You can make

your own drum from containers that you might find at home: cereal boxes, hat boxes, and round ice-cream cartons.

Drums can also be made from small wooden barrels or wooden salad bowls. Drumheads may be made by stretching old inner tubes or heavy fabric over the top of the drum body.

To make an Indian drum, you will need a container that is open at both ends. A drumhead must be attached at each end. The two heads may be laced together with leather strips or heavy shoelaces.

You may play a drum with a hard or soft drumstick. To make a soft drumstick, tie a clump of absorbent cotton around the end of a stick.

● Shakers

You can make a shaking rattling instrument by putting small objects into any kind of container. The rattling objects can be pebbles, wooden beads, dried beans, or grains of rice.

Rain rattles may be made by fastening small shells or tiny pieces of metal to a stick. The small objects will jingle when the stick is shaken.

A HOME OUTDOORS

The American cowboy often made his home outdoors.
In this song, a cowboy sings of the beauty of that home.

Home on the Range

American Cowboy Song

1. Oh, give me a home where the buf - fa - lo roam,
2. How of - ten at night when the heav - ens are bright

Where the deer and the an - te - lope play, _____
With the lights from the glit - ter - ing stars, _____

Where sel - dom is heard a dis - cour - ag - ing word,
Have I stood there a - mazed and ___ asked as I gazed,

And the skies are not cloud - y all day. _____
If their glo - ry ex - ceeds that of ours. _____

REFRAIN

Home, home on the range, _____

Where the deer and the an - te - lope play, _____

Where sel - dom is heard a dis - cour - ag - ing word,

And the skies are not cloud - y all day. _____

Open Range

Prairie goes to the mountain,
  Mountain goes to the sky.
The sky sweeps across to the distant hills
And here, in the middle,
  Am I.

Hills crowd down to the river,
  River runs by the tree.
Tree throws its shadow on sunburnt grass
And here, in the shadow,
  Is me.

Shadows creep up the mountain,
  Mountain goes black on the sky,
The sky bursts out with a million stars
And here, by the campfire,
  Am I.

Kathryn and Byron Jackson

EASY RIDER

This is a song that was sung by someone who went out west to become a cowhand. Although the work was hard, he decided to settle down in Montana.

My Home's in Montana

American Cowboy Song   Words Adapted by W. S. Williams

1. My home's in Mon - tan - a, I left In - di - an - a
2. I learned how to las - so Way down in El Pa - so,

To start a new life Far a - way in the West;
I've fol - lowed the cat - tle Wher - ev - er they roam;

My skin's rough as leath - er, Made tough by the weath - er;
I'm wear - y of stray - ing, Right here I'll be stay - ing,

The wind and the sun Of the land I love best.
I'll wan - der no more For Mon - tan - a's my home.

● Play a Part

Choose one of these patterns to accompany "My Home's in Montana." Which pattern will you choose? Play it all through the song.

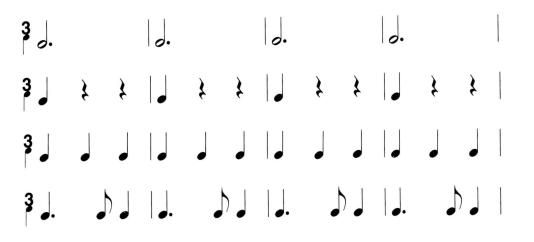

A Cowhand's Lullaby

Motherless calves are called *dogies*. The cowhand sings to the dogies to quiet them at night. If you were a cowhand, how would you use your voice to quiet the dogies?

Night Herding Song

American Cowboy Song

1. Oh, slow up, do - gies, quit rov - ing a - round,

You have wan - dered and tram - pled all o - ver the ground;

Oh, graze a - long, do - gies, and feed kind - a slow,

And don't for - ev - er be on the go.

Oh, move slow, do - gies, move slow, _____

Hi - oo, hi - oo, _____ hi - oo! _____

2. I've circle herded and night herded too,
But to keep you together, that's what I can't do;
My horse is leg weary, and I'm awful tired,
But if you get away, I am sure to get fired.
Bunch up, little dogies, bunch up,
Hi-oo, hi-oo, hi-oo!

3. Oh, lie still, dogies, since you have lain down,
Stretch away out on the big open ground;
Snore loud, little dogies, and drown the wild sound,
That will all go away when the day rolls round.
Lie still, little dogies, lie still.
Hi-oo, hi-oo, hi-oo!

Bell Part

Use the bells to play the *Hi-oo* parts
at the end of each verse.

The letters under the bell part will tell
you which bells you will need.

F   A   G

UNDER THE BIG TOP

Aaron Copland, a famous American composer, wrote the music for a movie called *The Red Pony*. The movie is about a ten-year-old boy named Jody, who received a red pony as a gift from his father. Jody loved his pony and often dreamed about the wonderful things they could do together. In one of his dreams, Jody was a ringmaster at a circus, putting his pony through his act.

Here is the music Copland wrote for Jody's imaginary day at the circus. Does the music sound like circus music to you?

"Circus Music" from *The Red Pony* .. Copland

Listening for the Theme

Here is a melody, or **theme**, that Copland used in his "Circus Music." Do you hear the theme in section A or in section B?

Aaron Copland
(1900–1990)

Meet the Composer

Although Aaron Copland grew up in Brooklyn, New York, people often think of him as a westerner because of some of the music he composed. In pieces such as *Billy the Kid* and *Rodeo,* Copland used American cowboy songs and old fiddle tunes. In fact, Copland described himself as a "cowboy from Brooklyn."

In addition to *The Red Pony,* Copland wrote music for several other movies. He composed music for the stage and concert hall as well. Aaron Copland is one of America's finest composers. His music is heard and loved by audiences all over the world.

A Sailor's Work Song

Sailors who worked on ships sang as they worked.
The songs they sang were called **shanties.** Pretend
that you are a sailor on board a clipper ship. Swab
the deck or hoist the sails in time to the music of this
old sea shantey.

Johnny, Come to Hilo

Sea Shantey

Oh, a poor old _ man came a - rid - ing _ by,

Says I "Old man, your _ horse will die."

Oh, John - ny, come to Hi - lo, oh, poor old man.

Oh, wake her, oh, shake her;

Oh, swing that girl with the blue dress on.

Oh, John - ny, come to Hi - lo, Oh, poor old man.

Clipper Ships and Captains

There was a time before our time,
It will not come again,
When the best ships still were wooden ships,
But the men were iron men.

The skippers with the little beards
And the New England drawl,
Who knew Hong Kong and Marblehead
And the Pole Star over all.

Stately as churches, swift as gulls,
They trod the oceans, then;
No man has seen such ships before
And none will see again.

Rosemary and Stephen Vincent Benet

A Song That Tells a Story

Many years ago, whaling ships sailed out of
Massachusetts. The work was very dangerous and the
journeys sometimes lasted for years. This is a song
sailors sang about their hard life at sea.

Blow, Ye Winds

American Folk Song

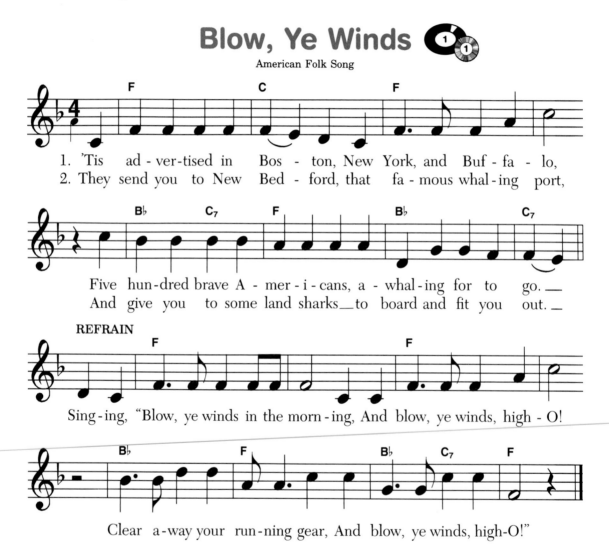

1. 'Tis ad-ver-tised in Bos-ton, New York, and Buf-fa-lo,
2. They send you to New Bed-ford, that fa-mous whal-ing port,

Five hun-dred brave A-mer-i-cans, a-whal-ing for to go. —
And give you to some land sharks—to board and fit you out. —

REFRAIN

Sing-ing, "Blow, ye winds in the morn-ing, And blow, ye winds, high - O!

Clear a-way your run-ning gear, And blow, ye winds, high-O!"

3. They tell you of the clipper ships
   a-going in and out,
   And say you'll take five hundred sperm
   before you're six months out.

4. It's now we're out to sea, my boys,
   the wind begins to blow,
   One half the watch is sick on deck
   and the other half below.

5. The skipper's on the quarter-deck
      a-squinting at the sails,
   When up aloft the look-out sights
      a school of whales.

6. "Now clear away the boats, my boys,
      and after him we'll trail,
   But if you get too near to him,
      he'll kick you with his tail!"

7. Now we've got him turned up,
      we tow him alongside;
   We over with our blubber hooks
      and rob him of his hide.

8. Next comes the stowing down, my boys;
      'twill take both night and day,
   And you'll all have fifty cents apiece
      when you collect your pay.

FISHERMAN'S SONG

Not long after America was discovered, fishing villages appeared along the rugged coast of Newfoundland. Here is a song that the fishermen sang when the long day's work was done.

As you listen to the song, pat your knees in time to the music.

I'se the B'y

Folk Song from Newfoundland   New Words and New Music Adaptation by Oscar Brand

1. I'se the b'y that builds the boat, I'se the b'y that sails her.

I'se the b'y that catch-es the fish And brings them home to Li - za.

REFRAIN

Swing your part-ner, Sal - ly Tib-ble, Swing your part-ner, Sal - ly Brown.

Swing your part-ner, ev - 'ry-one, All a - round the cir - cle.

2. I took Liza to the dance;
   Faith, but she could travel.
   Ev'ry step that Liza took
   Covered an acre of gravel.

3. Susan White is out of sight,
   Hiding like Jack Horner.
   Choose a lad and take him back,
   Kiss him in the corner.

Two Patterns to Play

Can you find these patterns in "I'se the B'y"? Try playing one of the patterns as the class sings the song.

AN OLD FAVORITE

The picture in your book shows one way that people used to travel between Albany and Buffalo—two cities in New York State.

This old song was a favorite with people everywhere, but especially with those who worked on the Erie Canal. Join in on the refrain when you can.

Buffalo Gals

American Minstrel Song

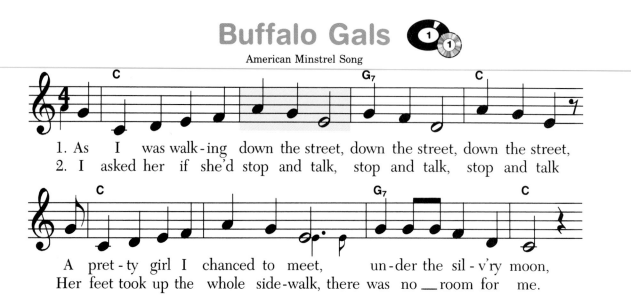

1. As I was walk-ing down the street, down the street, down the street,
2. I asked her if she'd stop and talk, stop and talk, stop and talk

A pret-ty girl I chanced to meet, un-der the sil-v'ry moon,
Her feet took up the whole side-walk, there was no ___ room for me.

REFRAIN

Oh, Buf-fa-lo gals won't you come out to-night,

come out to-night, come out to-night,

Oh, Buf-fa-lo gals won't you come out to-night

And dance by the light of the moon?

3. I asked her if she'd care to walk,
   care to walk, care to walk,
   She said she'd rather stand and talk,
   Oh, she was fair to see. *Refrain*

4. I asked her if she'd care to dance,
   care to dance, care to dance,
   She said that she would take a chance
   And shake a foot with me. *Refrain*

● Autoharp Strum

You can play an accompaniment for "Buffalo Gals" with
only two autoharp chords. Try this strumming pattern.

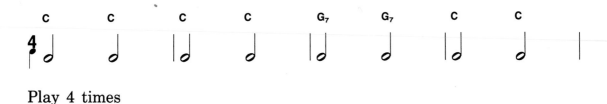

Play 4 times

RAILROAD TALK

Dummy is the nickname for a small, slow train. These dummies used to stop at every cow barn to pick up milk for the city markets.

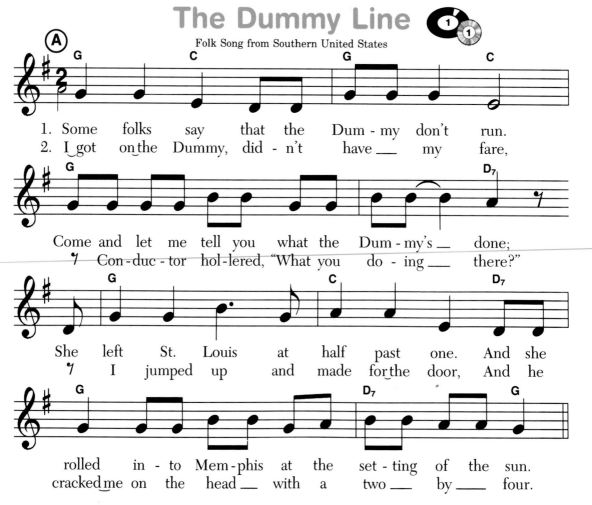

The Dummy Line

Folk Song from Southern United States

1. Some folks say that the Dum-my don't run.
2. I got on the Dummy, did-n't have my fare,

Come and let me tell you what the Dum-my's done;
Con-duc-tor hol-lered, "What you do-ing there?"

She left St. Louis at half past one. And she
I jumped up and made for the door, And he

rolled in-to Mem-phis at the set-ting of the sun.
cracked me on the head with a two by four.

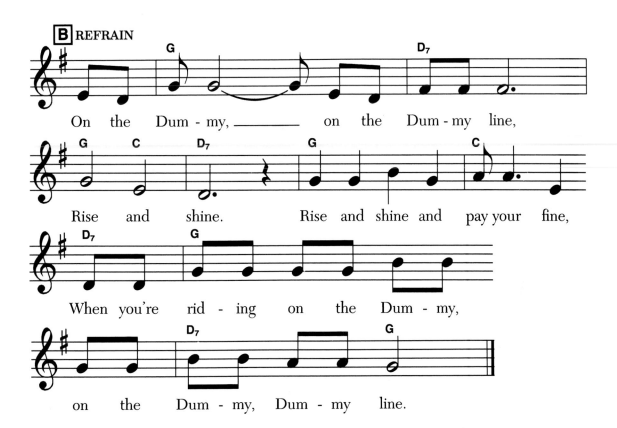

On the Dum - my, _____ on the Dum - my line,
Rise and shine. Rise and shine and pay your fine,
When you're rid - ing on the Dum - my,
on the Dum - my, Dum - my line.

3. I hopped off the Dummy and I lit on the track,
Dragged my feet and scraped my back.
I came to life and slung my dogs,
Looked for sure like I'm on the hog. *Refrain*

4. Some folks say that the Dummy don't run;
Come and let me tell you what the Dummy's done.
She left St. Louis at half-past two,
But I walked to Memphis 'fore the Dummy came through. *Refrain*

Can you find this **melody pattern** in the song?
Can you sing it? Can you play it on the bells?

Listen for the little train in this recording. How does
the music describe the little train's journey?

Train Ride . . . . Anonymous

OLD AMERICAN FOLK SONG

"Old Joe Clark" is as much fun to sing today as it was in the old pioneer days.

There are two different sections in this song. Can you tell where one section ends and the other one begins?

Old Joe Clark

American Folk Song   Words by Raymond Matthews

1. Old Joe Clark, he built a house, Took him 'bout a week;

He built the floors a-bove his head, The ceil-ings un-der his feet.

REFRAIN

Rock - a-rock, Old Joe Clark, Rock - a-rock, I'm gone;

Rock - a-rock, Old Joe Clark, Good-by, Lu-cy Long.

2. Old Joe Clark, he had a dog
   Like none you've ever seen;
   With floppy ears and curly tail,
   And six feet in between. *Refrain*

3. Old Joe Clark, he had a wife,
   Her name was Betty Sue;
   She had two great big brown eyes,
   The other two were blue. *Refrain*

● New Verses for Old Tunes

People have been making up new verses about old Joe Clark for years. Try singing these verses, then make up one of your own.

1. Old Joe Clark had a chicken coop
   Eighteen stories high,
   Every chicken in that coop
   Turned into chicken pie.

2. Old Joe Clark he had a cat,
   His tail was ten feet long,
   He wriggled his ears, and laid them flat,
   And sang a mournful song.

SQUARE-DANCE TUNE

"Pop, Goes the Weasel" was a favorite square-dance tune of the pioneers.

What instruments accompany the voices in the recording of this toe-tapping song?

Pop, Goes the Weasel

American Square Dance Tune

1.   All   a-round the cob - blers bench,   Mon-key chased the wea-sel,
2. The paint-er needs a   lad-der and brush, The art - ist needs an   ea-sel.

Mon - key thought 'twas all __ in   fun,   Pop,   goes the wea - sel.
Danc-ers   need   a   fid - dler's tune,   Pop,   goes the wea - sel.

Pen - ny for   a   spool __ of thread,   Pen - ny for   a   nee - dle,
I've no time to   wait or to sigh, No pa-tience to wait till by and by,

That's the way   the mon - ey goes,   Pop,   goes the wea - sel.
Kiss   me quick, I'm off, good-bye,   Pop,   goes the wea - sel.

Listen for square-dance music played by an orchestra.

"Hoe-Down" from *Rodeo* . . . . Copland

JUMBLED AND JIVEY

Follow the words of this song as you listen to the recording. You may not find out what *Mairzy Doats* means until the middle of the song.

Mairzy Doats

By Milton Drake, Al Hoffman and Jerry Livingston

Mair - zy doats and do - zy doats and lid - dle lam - zy div - ey,

A kid - dle - y div - ey too, would - n't you? Yes!

Mair - zy doats and do - zy doats and lid - dle lam - zy div - ey,

A kid - dle - y div - ey too, would - n't you?

If the words sound queer, and fun - ny to your ear,

A lit - tle bit jum - bled and jiv - ey, Sing

"Mares eat oats and does eat oats and lit - tle lambs eat i - vy."

Oh! Mair - zy doats and do - zy doats and lid - dle lam - zy div - ey,

A kid - dle - y div - ey too, would - n't you? ____

Eletelephony

Once there was an elephant,
Who tried to use the telephant—
No! no! I mean an elephone
Who tried to use the telephone—
(Dear me! I am not certain quite
That even now I've got it right.)

Howe'er it was, he got his trunk
Entangled in the telephunk;
The more he tried to get it free,
The louder buzzed the telephee—
(I fear I'd better drop the song
Of elephop and telephong!)

Laura E. Richards

NOAH'S ARK

There are many folk songs about Noah and the ark. In this humorous song, one singer can sing the solo parts. The class can join in on the chorus parts.

One More River

American Folk Song

Solo

1. Old No-ah built him-self an ark,
2. The an-i-mals came two by two,

Chorus

There's one more riv-er to cross,

Solo

He built it out of hick-'ry bark,
The el-e-phant and kan-ga-roo,

Chorus

One more riv-er to cross. _

One more riv-er, And that one riv-er is Jor-dan,

One more riv-er, There's one more riv-er to cross. _

3. The animals came three by three,
    There's one more river to cross,
    The baboon and the chimpanzee,
    There's one more river to cross . . .

4. The animals came four by four, . . .
    Old Noah got mad and hollered for more, . . .

5. The animals came five by five, . . .
    The bees came swarming from the hive, . . .

6. The animals came six by six, . . .
    The lion laughed at the monkey's tricks, . . .

7. When Noah found he had no sail, . . .
    He just ran up his old coat tail, . .

A TONGUE TWISTER

The chicken in this song found something new to say.
Listen to the recording to find out what she said.

When the chicken starts to sing her new song, clap
the steady beat in time to the music.

Chickery Chick

Words and Music by Sylvia Dee and Sidney Lippman

Once there lived a chick-en who would say, "Chick-chick" "Chick-chick" all day.

Soon that chick got sick and tired of just "Chick-chick," —

So one morn-ing she start-ed to say:

"Chick-er-y chick cha-la cha-la, Check-a-la rome-y

in a ba-nan-i-ka, bol-i-ka wol-i-ka can't you see,

Chick-er-y Chick is me."

Ev - 'ry time you're sick and tired of just the same old thing,

Say - in' just the same old words all day,

Be just like the chick - en who found some-thing new to sing.

Op - en up your mouth and start to say, Oh!

A Musical Conversation

This is a song that was written by the first black people to come to this country. It is called a spiritual, a kind of religious folk song. Listen to the recording to find out who sings the solo parts and who sings the chorus parts in this musical conversation.

Who Did?

African-American Spiritual

Who did swal-low Jo - Jo - Jo - Jo?

Who did swal-low Jo - nah? *Who did swal-low*

Jo - nah? Who did swal-low Jo - nah down? ____

2. Whale did, *Whale did,* Whale did, *Whale did,*
   Whale did swallow Jo-Jo-Jo-Jo.
   Whale did, *Whale did,* Whale did, *Whale did,*
   Whale did swallow Jo-Jo-Jo-Jo.
   Whale did, *Whale did,* Whale did, *Whale did,*
   Whale did swallow Jo-Jo-Jo-Jo.
   Whale did swallow Jonah,
   Whale did swallow Jonah,
   Whale did swallow Jonah up.

3. Daniel, *Daniel,* Daniel, *Daniel,*
   Daniel in the li-li-li-li. (3 times)
   Daniel in the lion's,
   Daniel in the lion's,
   Daniel in the lion's den.

4. Gabriel, *Gabriel,* Gabriel, *Gabriel,*
   Gabriel blow your trump-trump-trump-trump. (3 times)
   Gabriel blow your trumpet,
   Gabriel blow your trumpet,
   Gabriel blow your trumpet loud.

In this piece you will hear a musical conversation between two instruments. Can you name them?

Gavotte . . . . Bolling

A STORY IN MUSIC

Henri Rousseau, *The Equatorial Jungle* (detail), National Gallery of Art, Chester Dale Collection, Washington, D.C.

THE EQUATORIAL JUNGLE   *Henri Rousseau*

Maurice Ravel composed a group of pieces called *Mother Goose Suite,* which tells the story of some favorite fairy tales. We know that music cannot tell a story as words do or paint a picture in lines and colors that our real eyes can see. Music can only suggest—make us think of a story or picture.

What does this music suggest to you?

"The Conversations of Beauty and the Beast"
from *Mother Goose Suite* . . . . Ravel

The Conversation

At the beginning of the piece, you hear Beauty's voice.

Then the Beast speaks.

Can you hear the place in the music where Beauty and the Beast talk at the same time?

Meet the Composer

Maurice Ravel
(1875–1937)

Maurice Ravel was born in southwestern France in 1875. Maurice learned to play the piano when he was still a child. As he grew older he became fascinated with the instruments of the orchestra. He wanted to know how each instrument worked—how it sounded, how high and how low it could play. Ravel was also interested in composing, and before he was 20 years old, he began writing music of his own.

Mother Goose Suite was first written for piano. Later on, when Ravel rewrote the piece for orchestra, he was careful to choose the instrument that would best suit each character in his musical story.

A SOLO-CHORUS SONG

Listen to the solo parts and join in on the chorus parts.

All Night, All Day

African-American Spiritual

Can you find this pattern in the song?
Can you play it on the bells?
The pattern starts on the D bell.

ADD A VERSE

Look at the music in the color box. Can you find another phrase that looks exactly like it?

He's Got the Whole World in His Hands

African-American Spiritual

1. He's got the whole world in his hands, —
He's got the whole world in his hands, —
He's got the whole world in his hands, —
He's got the whole world in his hands. _____

2. He's got the wind and rain in his hands, (3 times)
   He's got the whole world in his hands.

3. He's got both you and me in his hands, (3 times)
   He's got the whole world in his hands.

4. He's got everybody in his hands, (3 times)
   He's got the whole world in his hands.

Make up a new verse to sing with the melody of "He's Got the Whole World in His Hands." Teach your classmates to sing your new verse.

CAREERS IN MUSIC

Kim and Reggie Harris make music in many places. These pictures show them in a studio, on a stage, and in a classroom.

BICYCLE BUILT FOR TWO

This song has been a favorite for almost 100 years.
Heads still turn when a bicycle built for two goes by.

Daisy Bell

Words and Music by Harry Dacre

Dai - sy, Dai - sy, Give me your an - swer, do; _____

I'm half cra - zy, All for the love of you. _____

It won't be a styl - ish mar - riage; _____

I can't af - ford a car - riage, _____

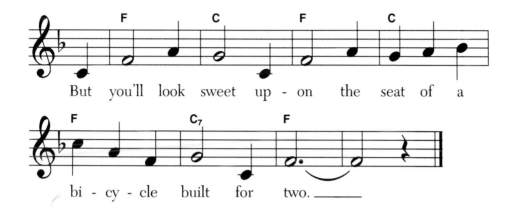

But you'll look sweet up - on the seat of a

bi - cy - cle built for two. _____

● Percussion Accompaniment

The woodblock and triangle can play an "oom-pah-pah" accompaniment for "Daisy Bell." Which part will you try? Team up with a friend and practice on your own.

Woodblock

Triangle

A Song About Smiles

When you smile, it usually means you are happy. When you smile, you make other people happy, too. Put a smile in your voice when you sing this happy song.

Smile That Smile

Words and Music by Carmino Ravosa

Smile that smile, You can, I know you.

Smile that smile, Don't let things throw you.

Smile that smile, Just look, I'll show you that way. _____

Laugh that laugh, Just let me hear it.

© 1985 Carmino Ravosa

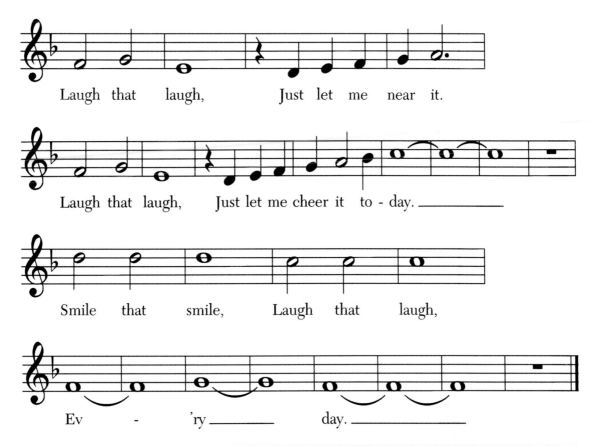

Laugh that laugh, Just let me near it.

Laugh that laugh, Just let me cheer it to-day. _____

Smile that smile, Laugh that laugh,

Ev - 'ry _____ day. _____

● Find the Melody Pattern

How many times do you see this melody pattern in "Smile that Smile"? Use the bells and play the pattern every time it comes in the song.

F   G   E

A SONG THAT NEVER ENDS

This is a song from a movie called *Bambi*. Bambi was a fawn who lived in the forest with a rabbit named Thumper and a skunk named Flower.

At the beginning of the movie, all the creatures of the forest are living happily together, and this is the song they sing.

Love Is a Song

Words by Larry Morey   Music by Frank Churchill

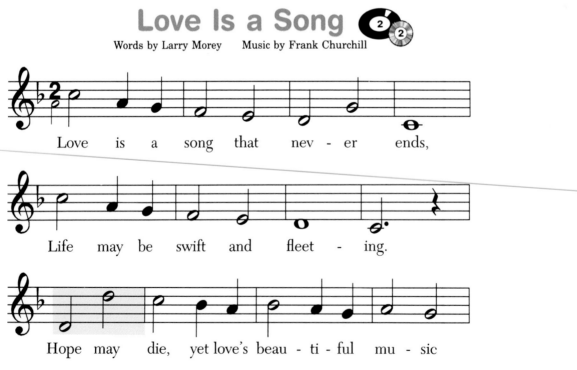

Love   is   a   song   that   nev - er   ends,

Life   may   be   swift   and   fleet - ing.

Hope   may   die,   yet love's beau - ti - ful   mu - sic

comes each day like the dawn. _____

Love is a song that nev - er ends;

One sim - ple theme re - peat - ing.

Like the voice of a heav - en - ly choir, _

love's sweet mu - sic flows on. _____

The Message of the Bells

There are many churches in London. Most of the churches have big bells in their towers. For hundreds of years these bells have been ringing out the time of day or announcing important events.

In the old days, people heard the bells clearly. Can you think of why it might be harder to hear them today?

Oranges and Lemons

Traditional Song from England

1. Or-an-ges and lem-ons, say the bells of St. Clem-ent's;

You owe me five far-things, say the bells of St. Mar-tin's;

When will you pay me? say the bells of Old Bai-ley;

When I grow rich, say the bells of Shore-ditch;

When will that be? — say the bells of Step - ney; —

I do not know — says the great bell of Bow.

2. Pancakes and fritters, say the bells of St. Peter's;
   Two sticks and an apple, say the bells of Whitechapel;
   Old Father Baldpate, say the slow bells of Aldgate;
   Poker and tongs, say the bells of St. John's;
   Kettles and pans, say the bells of St. Ann's;
   Brickbats and tiles, say the bells of St. Giles.

● Westminster-Chime Pattern

Can you play this pattern on the bells? You
will need the low-C, F, G, and A bells.

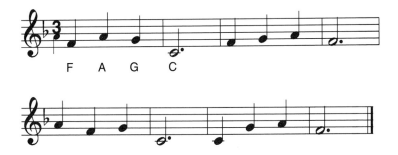

F   A   G   C

Try tolling the hour on a low-C bell.

Now try this. Using the same four bells,
try making up a bell pattern of your own.

BELL INTRODUCTIONS

Listen for the bell tune that is played as an introduction to this song. The tune is played on handbells.

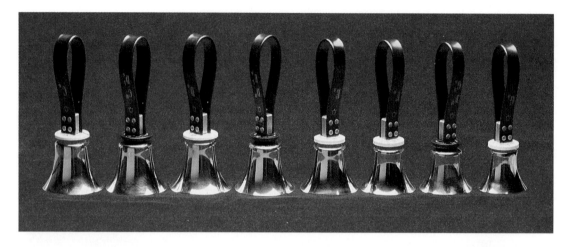

The Little Bells of Westminster

Traditional Round

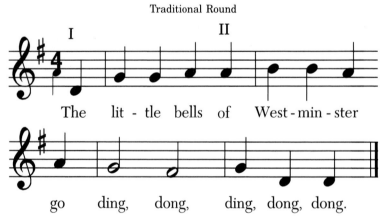

The lit-tle bells of West-min-ster go ding, dong, ding, dong, dong.

Which bell tune will you play as an introduction to "The Little Bells of Westminster"?

EVENING BELLS

Play a ringing sound on a triangle or on the finger cymbals to accompany this song.

Lovely Evening *(Fray Martin)*

Traditional Round

I

Oh, how love - ly is the eve - ning,
Fray Mar - tin al cam - pa - na - ri - o,

II

is the eve - ning, When the bells are
cam - pa - na - ri - o, Su - bey to - ca

sweet - ly ring - ing, sweet - ly ring - ing
la cam - pa - na, la cam - pa - na,

III

Ding, dong, ding, dong, ding, dong!
Tan, tan, tan, tan, tan, tan!

A CHANT FROM HAWAII

Hawaiians welcome newcomers to their islands with the greeting *Aloha*.

As you listen to the recording, use your arm to draw a rainbow shape in the air for each line of the song.

Alekoki

Hawaiian Chant   English Version by Aura Kontra

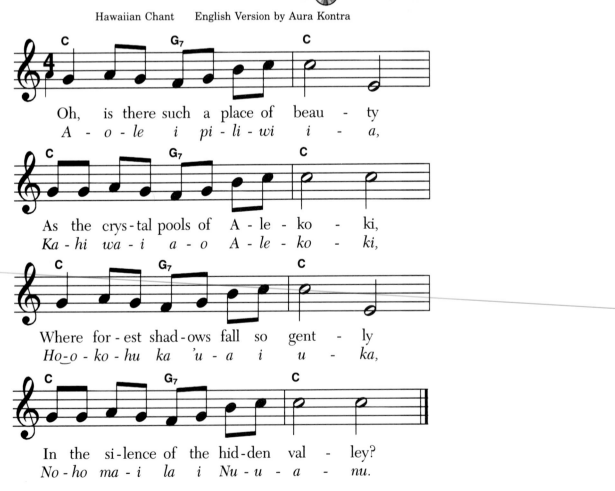

Oh, is there such a place of beau - ty
A - o - le i pi - li - wi i - a,

As the crys - tal pools of A - le - ko - ki,
Ka - hi wa - i a - o A - le - ko - ki,

Where for - est shad - ows fall so gent - ly
Ho - o - ko - hu ka 'u - a i u - ka,

In the si - lence of the hid - den val - ley?
No - ho ma - i la i Nu - u - a - nu.

SONG OF THE BURRITO

The *burrito* in this song can walk, talk, and even eat with a fork!

Tinga Layo

Calypso from the West Indies   English Version by Margaret Marks

REFRAIN

Tin - ga Lay - o!   Run, lit - tle don - key, run!
¡Ven, mi bu - rri - to, ven!

Tin - ga Lay - o!   Run, lit - tle don - key, run! run!
¡Ven, mi bu - rri - to, ven! ven!

1.–3. | Last time only

VERSE

1. My don - key yes, my don - key no,
1. *Bu - rri - to sí, bu - rri - to no.*

My don - key stop when I tell him to go!
¡Bu - rri - to co - me con te - ne - dor!

2. My donkey hee, my donkey haw,
    My donkey sit on the kitchen floor! *Refrain*

3. My donkey kick, my donkey balk,
    My donkey eat with a silver fork! *Refrain*

LULLABY FROM PUERTO RICO

A **lullaby** is a love song sung by a mother to her child.
Can you think of a word that will tell how a lullaby
should be sung?

Go to Sleep, My Treasure

Folk Song from Puerto Rico

1. Oh, go to sleep, my trea - sure, Oh, go to sleep, my trea - sure,
2. Oh, hush - a - by, my ba - by, Oh, hush - a - by, my ba - by,
   Du - er - ma - se, ri - cu - ra, Du - er - ma - se, mi ni - no,

For all the lit - tle an - gels are watch - ing from the skies. __
For all the lit - tle an - gels are watch - ing ov - er you. __
Que los __ an - ge - li - tos Mi - ran - do - te es - tan. __

Oh, go to sleep, my trea - sure, Oh, go to sleep, my trea - sure,
Oh, hush - a - by, my ba - by, Oh, hush - a - by, my ba - by,
Du - er - ma - se, ri - cu - ra, Du - er - ma - se, mi ni - nõ,

The night is grow - ing dark, and it's time to close your eyes. ___
The lit - tle guar - dian an - gels will watch the whole night through. _
Que la no - che ob - scu - ra, Du - er - ma - se, ri - cu - ra.

From **LULLABIES OF** THE WORLD, by Dorothy Berliner Commins. Copyright © 1967 by Dorothy Berliner Commins. Reprinted by permission of Random House, **Inc.**

Listen for the lullaby melody in this piece.

Trumpeter's Lullaby . . . . Anderson

FIESTA TIME

On the seventh of July, people of Spanish origin sing this song to celebrate the fiesta in honor of the Spanish Saint Fermin.

The First of January (Uno de enero)

Folk Song from Mexico

A

First of the first month, sec-ond of the sec-ond month, Third of the
U - no de̲e - ne - ro, dos __ de fe - bre - ro, tres __ de

third, and fourth of the fourth; Fifth of the fifth month, sixth of the
mar - zo, cua - tro de̲a - bril, cin - co de ma - yo, seis __ de

sixth month, Sev-enth of Ju - ly is San Fer - min.
ju - nio, sie - te de ju - lio, San Fer - mín.

B

La, la, la, la, la, la, la, Tam-bour-ine's brok-en, we can-not play it.
¿quién__ ha ro - to la pan - de - re - ta?

La, la, la, la, la, la, la, If you broke it, you must re-place it.
el que la̲ha ro - to la pa - ga - rá. __

This song tells you how to count from one to seven in Spanish: *uno, dos, tres, cuatro, cinco, seis, siete.*

You will hear seven songs. When a number is called, listen to the music. Then on your worksheet, write a check mark in the blank after the correct answer.

1. It is a cowhand's song. _____
It is a sailor's song. _____

2. It is a song about farming. _____
It is a Native-American chant. _____

3. It is a railroad song. _____
It is a Native-American chant. _____

4. It is a song of the sea. _____
It is a song a cowhand sings. _____

5. It is a song about farming. _____
It is a song about a railroad. _____

6. It is a railroad song. _____
It is a song a cowhand sings. _____

7. It is a sailor's work song. _____
It is a Native-American chant. _____

TEST 1

After each number you will find words that describe a song in your book. From the song list, choose the song that fits each description and, on your worksheet, write its letter in the blank.

1. A song that was composed by Woody Guthrie ____

2. A song that comes from a Native-American tribe ____

3. A song that American cowhands sang ____

4. A song that is a sea shantey ____

5. A song that is used as an American square-dance tune ____

6. A song that has solo parts and chorus parts ____

7. A song that was sung by Norwegian farmers ____

8. A song that was sung by Newfoundland fishermen ____

A. I'se the B'y
B. Pop, Goes the Weasel
C. This Land Is Your Land
D. Oleana
E. My Home's in Montana
F. H'Atira
G. Johnny, Come to Hilo
H. One More River

TEST 2

After each song title you will find two words.
Circle the word that best describes how the song
should be sung.

1. This Land Is Your Land   joyfully   quietly

2. All Night, All Day   quietly   quickly

3. Blow, Ye Winds   calmly   energetically

4. Grandma's Farm   merrily   sadly

5. Old Joe Clark   sadly   cheerfully

6. Who Did?   slowly   lively

7. Chickery Chick   humorously   sadly

8. Buffalo Gals   lively   calmly

9. Daisy Bell   heavily   lightly

10. Love Is a Song   smoothly   jaggedly

You will hear selections from the Listening Library. When a number is called, read the sentence next to the number and listen to the music. If you think the statement is true, circle the word TRUE on your worksheet. If the statement is false, circle the word FALSE.

1. This is the beginning of Copland's "Circus Music."

TRUE   FALSE

2. This is the B section of "Circus Music"; it ends with loud chords.

TRUE   FALSE

3. This is Beauty's theme from "The Conversations of Beauty and the Beast."

TRUE   FALSE

4. This is Beauty's theme from "The Conversations of Beauty and the Beast."

TRUE   FALSE

5. In this music, the melody is played by a clarinet.

TRUE   FALSE

6. This music starts slow and gets faster.

TRUE   FALSE

7. In this music you hear a piano and a trumpet.

TRUE   FALSE

8. In this music the melody is played by a trumpet.

TRUE   FALSE

UNDERSTANDING MUSIC

TEMPO: FAST–SLOW

Which picture shows a
rider moving fast?

Which picture shows
riders moving slow?

Listen to this song. Which part is fast?
Which part is slow?

Stodola Pumpa

Czechoslovakian Folk Song   Words Adapted

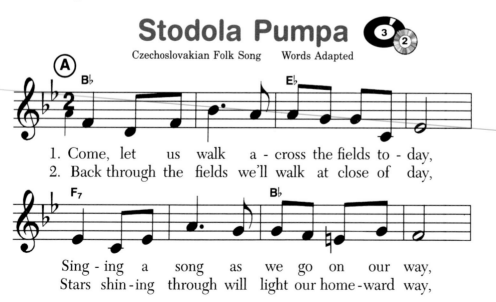

1. Come, let us walk   a - cross the fields to - day,
2. Back through the fields we'll walk at close of   day,

Sing - ing a   song   as   we go on   our way,
Stars shin - ing through will light our home - ward way,

Come, let us walk a - cross the fields to - day,
Back through the fields we'll walk at close of day

Sing - ing a song as we go on our way. — Hey!
Stars shin - ing through will light our home - ward way. —

B REFRAIN

Sto - do - la, sto - do - la, sto - do - la pum - pa,

Sto - do - la pum - pa, sto - do - la pum - pa,

Sto - do - la, sto - do - la, sto - do - la pum - pa,

Sto - do - la pum - pa, pum, pum, pum.

Listen to this music. Can you hear parts
that move fast and parts that move slow?

Hungarian Dance No. 6 . . . . Brahms

TEMPO: FASTER–SLOWER

Each of the objects pictured above can get faster and slower. Can you name other objects that can get faster and slower?

What happens to the **tempo** in this song? Does the music get faster? Slower?

Dancing

Czechoslovakian Folk Song

Come and dance, turn light-ly, turn light-ly,

A-round the camp-fire burn-ing so bright-ly,

The snow falls fast, and cold is the weath-er,

Come dance, come dance, we'll all turn to-geth-er.

La la la la, La la la la,

La la la la, La la la la la,

La la la la, La la la la,

La la la la, La la la la la la la la.

What happens to the tempo in this piece for
orchestra?

"Pizzicato Polka" from *Ballet Suite
No. 1* . . . . Shostakovich

STEADY BEAT

Pat your knees or clap your hands in time to the music of this lively song. You will be patting or clapping the steady beat.

I'd've Baked a Cake

Words and Music by Al Hoffman, Bob Merrill and Clem Watts

If I knew you were com-in' I'd-'ve baked a cake, —
Had you dropped me a let-ter I'd-'ve hired a band, —

baked a cake, — baked a cake, — If I
grand-est band — in the land, — Had you

knew you were com-in' I'd-'ve baked a cake, —
dropped me a let-ter I'd-'ve hired a band, —

1.
How-ja do, how-ja do, how-ja do.

2.
And spread the wel-come mat for you. ___

SETS OF TWO

Let your hands march left-right, left-right, as you listen to "The German Band." You might want to chant softly the words *left-right, left-right,* as the music goes along.

The German Band

German Folk Song   English Words by Margaret Marks

REFRAIN

Come and hear the Ger-man band, Ger-man band, Ger-man band!

Oh, the weath-er is so grand for the big pa - rade!

Fine

1. First there comes a drum-mer, And as a drum-mer,

He's quite a plumb-er! He's off the beat in ev - 'ry

D.C. al Fine

num-ber, And no one knows how come They let him drum. ___

2. Next come brasses playing,
   It sounds like neighing,
   Or donkeys braying!
   And all the people there are saying,
   "Let's stuff 'em up with hay
   So they won't play!" *Refrain*

3. Next comes our police force,
   Three men and one horse,
   I wonder who's boss!
   Although their leader shouts his head off,
   With his *a-hep, a-hep,*
   They're out of step! *Refrain*

● Pick a Pattern

You can chant or play an instrument to accompany
"The German Band." Will you chant or play?

Chant

Left right, left right, left right, left right,

Drum

Cymbals

Listen for beats in sets of two in this music.

LISTENING LIBRARY 4 3

"March" from *Nutcracker Suite* ....
.... Tchaikovsky

SETS OF TWO—METER IN 2

Which row of symbols shows the steady beat? Which row shows the beats in sets of two?

To feel the beats moving in sets of two, pretend to strum a banjo as you listen to this song. Strum down-up, down-up, across the strings.

Boil Them Cabbage Down

American Pioneer Song

1. The rac-coon's got a fur-ry tail,

The pos-sum's tail is bare, —

From MORE SONGS OF THE NEW WORLD by Desmond MacMahon. Published by Holmes McDougall Ltd.

The rab-bit ain't got no tail at all,

But a lit-tle bit o' bunch o' hair.

B REFRAIN

Boil them cab-bage down, down, Bake them bis-cuits brown, brown,

The on-ly tune I ev-er did learn is Boil them cab-bage down.

2. The June bug he has wings of gold,
   The firefly wings of flame,
   The bedbug's got no wings at all,
   But he gets there just the same. *Refrain*

3. Oh, love it is a killing fit
   When beauty hits a blossom,
   And if you want your finger bit,
   Just poke it at a possum. *Refrain*

⬤ Steady Beat—Strong Beat

Play the steady beat
on a woodblock.

Play the strong beat
on a drum.

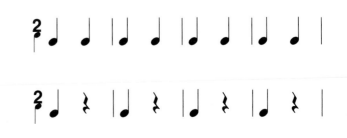

SETS OF THREE

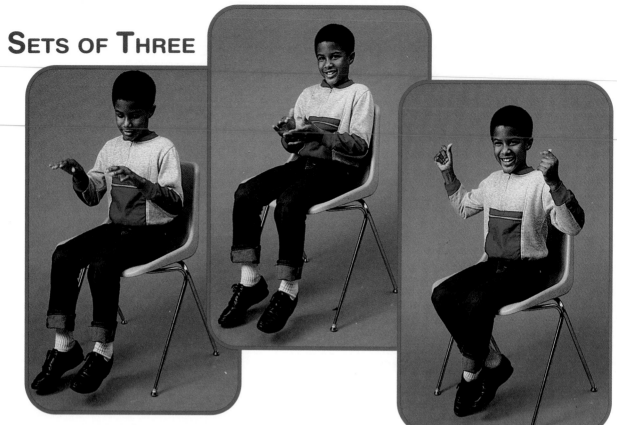

Make the hand motions shown in the pictures
as you listen to this old, favorite song.

Take Me Out to the Ball Game

Words by Jack Norworth   Music by Albert von Tilzer

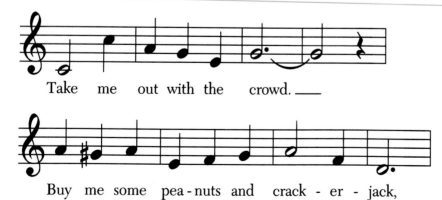

Take   me   out   to   the   ball   game,

Take   me   out with the   crowd. _____

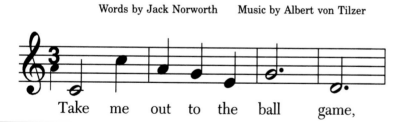

Buy   me   some   pea - nuts and   crack - er - jack,

I don't care if we nev-er get back,

Let me root, root, root for the home team,

If they don't win it's a shame, ___

For it's one, two, three strikes you're out

At the old ball game. ___

Pick a Pattern

Which pattern will you play to accompany the song?

Woodblock

Tambourine

Drum

Listen for beats in sets of three in this music.

"Waltz of the Doll" from *Coppelia*...Delibes

SETS OF THREE—METER IN 3

The top row of symbols shows the steady beat. What does the bottom row show?

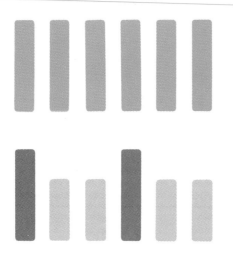

What sign tells you that this pattern moves in a meter of 3? Tap the pattern as you listen to "Springfield Mountain."

Springfield Mountain

American Folk Song

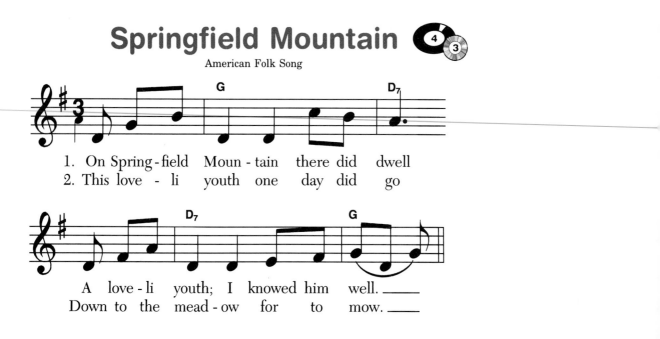

1. On Spring-field Moun-tain there did dwell
2. This love - li youth one day did go

A love - li youth; I knowed him well. ____
Down to the mead - ow for to mow. ____

Too loo - re - ay,   too   loo - re - oo,

Too loo - re - ay,   too   loo - re - oo.

3. He scarce had mowed quite round the field
   When a cruel sarpent bit his heel.

4. They took him home to Molli dear
   Which made him feel so very queer.

5. Now Molli had two ruby lips
   With which the p'ison she did sip.

6. Now Molli had a rotting tooth
   And so the p'ison killed them both.

● Steady Beat—Strong Beat

Play the steady beat on a woodblock.

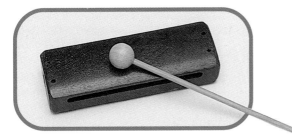

Play the strong beat on a drum.

SHORT SOUNDS–LONG SOUNDS

Follow the music as you listen to this song. Notice the notes in the color boxes. Do you hear the *Billy Boy* pattern anywhere else in the song?

Billy Boy

English Folk Song

1. Oh, __ where have you been, Bil - ly Boy, Bil - ly Boy?
2. Did she bid you to come in, Bil - ly Boy, Bil - ly Boy?

Oh, __ where have you been, charm-ing Bil-ly?   I have
Did she bid you to come in, charm-ing Bil-ly?   Yes, she

been to seek a wife, She's the joy __ of my life,
bid me to come in, There's a dim-ple in her chin,

She's a young thing and can-not leave her moth-er. _____

3. Did she give you a chair, Billy Boy, Billy Boy?
   Yes, she gave me a chair, but there was no bottom there,

4. Can she make a cherry pie, Billy Boy, Billy Boy?
   She can make a cherry pie, quick as a cat can wink her eye,

5. Can she cook and can she spin, Billy Boy, Billy Boy?
   She can cook and she can spin, she can do most anything,

6. How old is she, Billy Boy, Billy Boy?
   Three times six and four times seven, twenty-eight and eleven,

88   Rhythm

Chant, Clap, Play

CHANT the *Billy Boy* pattern several times.

Bil-ly Boy, Bil-ly Boy, Bil-ly Boy, Bil-ly Boy

CLAP the *Billy Boy* pattern several times. Say *short-short-long* as you clap.

▬ ▬ ▬▬ ▬ ▬ ▬ ▬▬ ▬ ▬ ▬ ▬▬ ▬

PLAY the *Billy Boy* pattern on a woodblock.

Chant a Pattern

1. John John Mar-y Mar-y
2. Car-los Car-los Jane Jane
3. Bet-ty Joe Bet-ty Joe
4. Jer-ry Jer-ry Jer-ry Beth

Play a Pattern

1.
2. 
3.
4.

Make up your own pattern of short and long sounds.

LONG–SHORT

Follow the music as you listen to the recording. Do the notes in the color boxes show long sounds or short sounds?

Louisiana Lullaby

Folk Song from Louisiana

1. Dream-land o-pens here,   Sweep the dream path clear.

Lis-ten child,   now lis-ten well,

What the tor-toise may have to tell,

What the tor-toise may have to tell.

2. Dreamland opens here,
   Sweep the dream path clear.
   Listen child, dear little child,
   To the song of the crocodile,
   To the song of the crocodile.

3. Dreamland opens here,
   Sweep the dream path clear.
   Listen child, now close your eyes,
   In the cane-break the wild cat cries,
   In the cane-break the wild cat cries.

Sound and Silence

In music, sounds are shown with notes.
Find these notes in "Louisiana Lullaby."

In music, silences are shown with rests.
Find these rests in "Louisiana Lullaby."

Look at the chart, and answer the questions below.

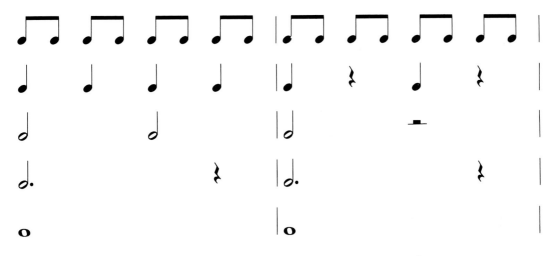

- How many eighth notes can take the place of a quarter note?

- How many quarter notes can take the place of a half note?

- How many quarter notes can take the place of a dotted half note?

- How many quarter notes can take the place of a whole note?

Listen for longer and shorter sounds in this music.

The Skater's Waltzes . . . . Waldteufel

HOW TONES MOVE: REPEATED TONES

Look at the notes in the color box. Do they move upward or downward, or do they stay the same?

Follow the music as you listen to the song. Can you find three other places where the tones repeat like those in the color box?

Deep in the Heart of Texas

Words by June Hershey   Music by Don Swander

The stars at night are big and bright,

Deep in the heart of Tex - as; _____

The prai - rie sky is wide and high,

Deep in the heart of Tex - as. _____

The sage in bloom is like per - fume,

Deep in the heart of Tex - as; _____

Re - minds me of the one I love,

Deep in the heart of Tex - as. _____

Play the repeated tones every time they come in the song.

Bells

C

How Tones Move: Upward by Step

Look at the notes in the color box. Do they move upward or downward, or do they stay the same?

Follow the music as you listen to the song. Can you find another place where the tones move upward by step like those in the color box?

Sheep Shearing

Swedish Folk Song   English Words by Sam Blum

VERSE

1. Go get the sheep, we're clip-ping to-day,
2. Tell Moth-er dear we're card-ing to-day,

Clip-ping their wool, yes, clip-ping their wool
Card-ing the wool, yes, card-ing the wool

So we can knit some stock-ings for you,
So we can knit a scarf for her, too,

Then we shall dance till morn-ing.
Then we shall dance till morn-ing.

REFRAIN

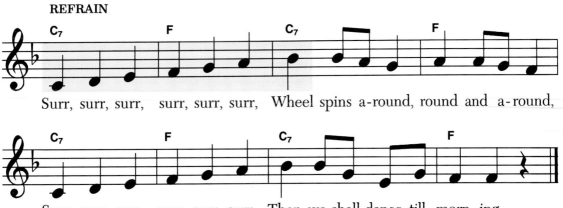

C₇ F C₇ F

Surr, surr, surr, surr, surr, surr, Wheel spins a-round, round and a-round,

C₇ F C₇ F

Surr, surr, surr, surr, surr, surr, Then we shall dance till morn-ing.

3. Tell brother John we're spinning today,
   Spinning the wool, yes, spinning the wool
   So we can knit a lace for his shoe,
   Then we shall dance till morning.

4. Tell sister Jane we're dyeing today,
   Dyeing the wool, yes, dyeing the wool
   So we can knit a sweater of blue,
   Then we shall dance till morning.

Play the tones that move upward by step every time they come in the song.

Bells

C B♭

How Tones Move: Downward by Step

Look at the notes in the color box. Do they move upward or downward, or do they stay the same?

Follow the music as you listen to the song. Can you find three other places where the tones move downward like those in the color box?

Nine Red Horsemen

Folk Melody from Mexico   Words by Eleanor Farjeon

1. I ___ saw nine red horse-men ride _ o - ver the plain,
2. Their _ hair streamed be - hind them, their _ eyes were a - shine;
3. Their _ spurs clinked and jin - gled, their _ laugh-ter was gay,

And _ each gripped his horse ___ by its long flow-ing mane.
They _ all rode as one man al - though they were nine.
And _ in the red sun - set they _ gal - loped a - way.

Ho hil-lo, hil-lo, hil-lo ho!   Ho hil-lo, hil-lo, hil-lo ho!

Ho hil-lo, hil-lo, hil-lo ho!   Ho hil-lo, hil-lo, hil-lo ho!

● Bell Patterns

The tones in each bell pattern move downward by step. Play each pattern then find it in the song.

Do you find the patterns in section A or in section B?

Bells

E

D

C

B

HOW TONES MOVE: UP AND DOWN BY LEAP

Look at the notes in the color box. Do they move by step, do they stay the same, or do they leap?

The Unbirthday Song

Words and Music by Mack David, Al Hoffman and Jerry Livingston

1. A ver-y mer-ry un-birth-day to you, to you.
2. A ver-y mer-ry un-birth-day to us, to us.

A ver - y mer-ry un-birth-day to you, to you.
A ver - y mer-ry un-birth-day to us, to us.

It's great to share with some-one and I guess that you will do;
If there are no ob - jec-tions, let it be u - nan - i - mous;

A ver - y mer-ry un - birth-day to you. _____
A ver - y mer-ry un - birth-day to us. _____

3. A very merry unbirthday to all, to all.
   A very merry unbirthday to all, to all.
   Let's have a celebration, hire a band and rent a hall;
   A very merry unbirthday to all.

Play the large leap downward
when it comes in the song.

Bells

C C

98 Melody

STEPS, LEAPS, REPEATS

Here are parts of songs you may know. Look at the music to see when the notes repeat, and when they move upward or downward by step or by leap. Try playing the parts on bells.

TWO PIECES FOR PIANO

The two pieces you will hear were composed by Robert Schumann. They are among the best-known and best-loved piano pieces of all time. Children play the pieces for family and friends. Famous pianists play the pieces in concert halls all over the world.

As you listen to the music, look at the words in the two lists below. Which list of words suggests the mood, or feeling, of the music in the first piece? In the second piece?

cheerful   quiet
jolly   peaceful
lively   restful

"The Happy Farmer" from *The Album for the Young* ....Schumann

"Dreaming" from *Scenes from Childhood* ... .Schumann

Here is the melody you hear at the beginning of "The Happy Farmer."

You hear this melody at the beginning of "Dreaming."

Robert Schumann
(1810–1856)

Meet the Composer

Just one year after Abraham Lincoln was born in Kentucky, a baby boy named Robert Schumann was born in a German village near Leipzig, which was at that time the music capital of the world. Lincoln grew up to be President of the United States; Schumann became one of Germany's finest composers.

Schumann studied piano with Herr Weick, one of the best piano teachers of his day. It was for Herr Weick's daughter Clara that Schumann wrote *Scenes from Childhood*, a series of 12 piano pieces, including "Traümerei" (the German word for *dreaming*).

FOLLOW THE PHRASE LINES

Notice the phrase lines above the music. As you listen to the recording, trace with your finger the rise and fall of each phrase line.

How many phrases does this melody have?

Down in the Valley

Kentucky Folk Song

1. Down in the val - ley, val - ley so low,
2. Build me a cas - tle for - ty feet high,

Hang your head o - ver, hear the wind blow,
So I can see you as you pass by.

Hear the wind blow, dear, hear the wind blow,
As you ride by, dear, as you ride by,

Hang your head o - ver, hear the wind blow.
So I can see you as you ride by.

3. Writing a letter, containing three lines,
   Answer my question: "Will you be mine?"
   Will you be mine, dear, will you be mine.
   Answer my question: "Will you be mine?"

PHRASE LENGTH

Follow the phrase lines as you listen to "Peace Like a River." Are the phrases all the same length, or are some long and some short?

Peace Like a River

Traditional

1. I've got peace like a riv-er,

I've got peace like a riv-er,

I've got peace like a riv-er in my soul.

I've got peace like a riv-er,

I've got peace like a riv-er,

I've got peace like a riv-er in my soul.

2. I've got joy like a fountain, *(2 times)*
   I've got joy like a fountain in my soul.
   I've got joy like a fountain, *(2 times)*
   I've got joy like a fountain in my soul.

3. I've got love like the ocean, *(2 times)*
   I've got love like the ocean in my soul.
   I've got love like the ocean, *(2 times)*
   I've got love like the ocean in my soul.

What can you discover about the phrases in this poem?

In Praise of Water

Water is a lovely thing:
Dark and ripply in a spring;
Black and quiet in a pool,
In a puddle brown and cool;
In a river blue and gay,
In a raindrop silver-gray;
In a fountain flashing white,
In a dewdrop crystal bright;
In a pitcher frosty-cold,
In a bubble pink and gold;
In a happy summer sea
Just as green as green can be;
In a rainbow, far unfurled,
Every color in the world.
All the year, from spring to spring,
Water is the loveliest thing!

Nancy Byrd Turner

MELODY AND HARMONY

You will hear two performances of a song in your book. As you listen to the recording, decide which picture shows what is happening in each performance.

LISTENING LIBRARY 5 3

America, Two Ways . . . . Traditional

Two Ways to Make Harmony

Look up the word *harmony* in the glossary on page 292 in your book. Then, add harmony to "Brother John" by playing chords on an autoharp. As the class sings the melody, play the F chord all through the song.

Brother John
(Frère Jacques)

Traditional French Round

Are you sleep-ing, Are you sleep-ing?
Frè - re Jac - ques, Frè - re Jac - ques,

Broth - er John, Broth - er John?
Dor - mez vous, Dor - mez vous?

Morn-ing bells are ring-ing, Morn-ing bells are sing-ing,
Son-nez les ma - ti - nes, Son-nez les ma - ti - nes,

Ding ding dong, Ding ding dong.
Din din don, Din din don.

● Ostinatos

Add harmony by singing or playing a repeated pattern (ostinato) all through the song. As the class sings the melody, try one of these ostinatos.

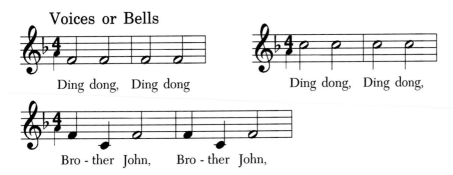

Voices or Bells

Ding dong, Ding dong

Ding dong, Ding dong,

Bro - ther John, Bro - ther John,

PARTNER SONGS

Listen to the recording of two American folk songs. One is printed on this page; the other, on the next page. Follow the music of each song as you listen.

Sandy Land

Folk Song from Oklahoma

1. Make my liv-in' in sand-y land,
Make my liv-in' in sand-y land,
Make my liv-in' in sand-y land,
La-dies, fare you well.

2. Raise sweet potatoes in sandy land, *(3 times)*
    Ladies, fare you well.

3. Dig sweet potatoes in sandy land, *(3 times)*
    Ladies, fare you well.

4. Make my livin' in sandy land, *(3 times)*
    Ladies, fare you well.

Add harmony to the melody of "Sandy Land" by playing the autoharp chords.

Bow, Belinda

American Singing Game

1. Bow, bow, bow, Be-lin-da;

Bow, bow, bow, Be-lin-da;

Bow, bow, bow, Be-lin-da;

You're the one, my dar-ling.

2. Right hand round, Oh, Belinda; *(3 times)*
   You're the one, my darling.

3. Left hand round, Oh, Belinda; *(3 times)*
   You're the one, my darling.

4. Both hands round, Oh, Belinda; *(3 times)*
   You're the one, my darling.

● Putting Two Songs Together

While some of your classmates sing "Sandy Land," others can sing "Bow, Belinda."

Singing partner songs is one way to create harmony.

FOLLOW THE LEADER

Listen for the voices playing follow-the-leader in the recording of this song.

Make New Friends

Round

Make new friends, but keep _ the _ old, ___

One is sil - ver and the oth - er gold.

When your class can sing the melody of "Make New Friends" without the recording, try singing the song as a two-part round.

A Two-Part Round

When your class knows the melody of "Scotland's Burning," divide into two groups and sing the song as a two-part round.

Scotland's Burning
Round

I
Scot-land's burn-ing, Scot-land's burn-ing,

II
Look out, Look out, Fire! Fire! Fire! Fire!

Pour on wa - ter, Pour on wa - ter!

● Add an Ostinato

Add an ostinato to a performance of "Scotland's Burning." Will you sing the ostinato, or play it on the bells?

Wa - ter, Wa - ter

TWO MELODIES TOGETHER

Harmony is created when two melodies are sung at the same time. Listen for the harmony part on this recording of "Sandy Land."

Sandy Land

Folk Song from Oklahoma

1. Make my liv-in' in sand-y land,
Make my liv-in' in sand-y land,
Make my liv-in' in sand-y land,
La-dies, fare you well.

2. Raise sweet potatoes in sandy land, *(3 times)*
Ladies, fare you well.

3. Dig sweet potatoes in sandy land, *(3 times)*
Ladies, fare you well.

4. Make my livin' in sandy land, *(3 times)*
Ladies, fare you well.

Reprinted by permission of Curtis Brown, Ltd. Copyright © 1937, 1963 by B. A. Botkin.

Countermelody

Sand-y land, Sand-y land, Sand-y land, Fare you well.

ADD A COUNTERMELODY

Listen for the countermelody in the recording of "Roll on the Ground."

Roll on the Ground

Folk Song from Mississippi

REFRAIN

Roll on   the ground, boys,   roll on   the ground,

Roll on   the ground, boys,   roll on   the ground.

VERSE

1. Work on   the rail - road,   sleep on   the ground,
2. Work on   the rail - road,   work all   the day,

D.C. al Fine

Eat so - dy crack - ers, and the wind blow them a - round.
Eat so - dy crack - ers, and the wind blow them a - way.

Transcribed and Adapted from the Library of Congress Field Recordings AFS 2594.

Countermelody

Roll   on,   roll   on,   Roll   on, roll on.

TWO DIFFERENT SECTIONS

These pictures show you two things you will need
to make carrot stew.

Can you find the signs that tell you this song has
two different sections?

Carrot Stew

Words and Music by Larry Groce

Ⓐ VERSE

1. When - ev - er we have a friend for lunch,

There's just one thing to do. ___

We pick some ber - ries and catch some fish,

And we make a car-rot stew.

B REFRAIN

Car-rot stew, car-rot stew,

It's our fav'-rite thing— to do.

Get a pot and a car-rot or two,

And cook up a car-rot stew.

2. Nothing makes our tummies so full
And keeps us happy too,
As a great big pot or a little bitty bowl
Or a spoonful of carrot stew. *Refrain*

3. So when you come to our little house,
Bring a carrot if you have a few.
We'll put it in a pot 'til it's nice and hot,
And make some carrot stew. *Refrain*

Listen for two different sections in this piece for orchestra.

The Comedians................Kabalevsky

AB FORM

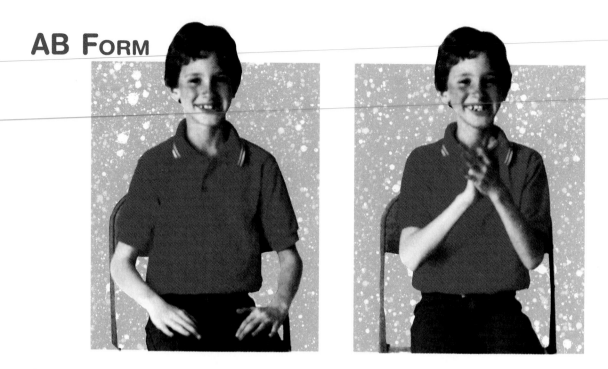

Listen for the two sections in this song.

Hop Up, My Ladies

American Folk Song

A

C   C

1. Did you ev-er go to meet-ing, Un-cle Joe, Un-cle Joe?

C   G₇

Did you ev-er go to meet-ing, Un-cle Joe? —

C   C

Did you ev-er go to meet-ing, Un-cle Joe, Un-cle Joe?

F   G₇   C

Don't mind the weath-er, so the wind don't blow.

Hop up, my la - dies, three in a row,

Hop up, my la - dies three in a row,

Hop up, my la - dies three in a row,

Don't mind the weath - er so the wind don't blow.

2. Will your horse carry double, Uncle Joe, Uncle Joe?
   Don't mind the weather, so the wind don't blow. *Refrain*

3. Is your horse a single-footer, Uncle Joe, Uncle Joe?
   Don't mind the weather, so the wind don't blow. *Refrain*

**Do you find this rhythm pattern in section A
or in section B?**

Hop up, my la - dies

Clap the pattern every time it comes in the song.

SHAPES AND LETTERS

1.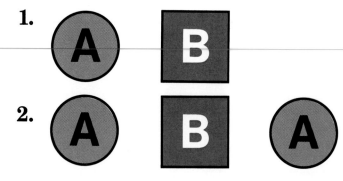

2.

Listen to the recording of "Hand Me Down." Which set of shapes and letters shows the form of the song?

Hand Me Down

A *Chorus*
African-American Spiritual

Oh, hand me down, Hand me down,

Hand me down my sil-ver trum-pet, Ga-briel.

Hand me down, throw it down, An-y way to get it down,

Hand me down my sil - ver trum-pet, Lord.

B *Solo*

Oh, Mo-ses had a lot to do, __

Listen for the two different sections in this piece for brass instruments. The chart will help you hear the form.

Trumpet Tune . . . . Purcell

1   Ⓐ

2   Ⓐ

3   ⬜B

4   ⬜B

Can you hear two different sections in this piece? Follow the chart as you listen.

"Ronde" from *Three Dances* . . . . Susato

1   Ⓐ

2   Ⓐ

3   ⬜B

4   ⬜B

CALL CHART 2

Following the chart will help you hear repetition and contrast in this piece for guitar.

Adelita (Mazurka)................Tárrega

1 Ⓐ

2 Ⓐ   (repetition)

3 B   (contrast)

4 Ⓐ   (repetition)

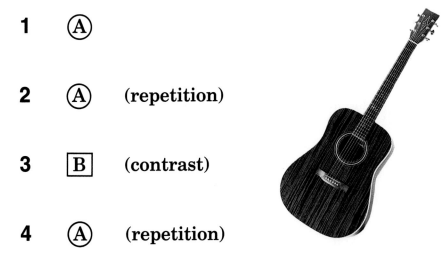

Can you hear repetition and contrast in this piece for piano? Follow the chart as you listen.

Preludes for Piano, No. 2.........Gershwin

1 Ⓐ

2 B   (contrast)

3 Ⓐ   (repetition)

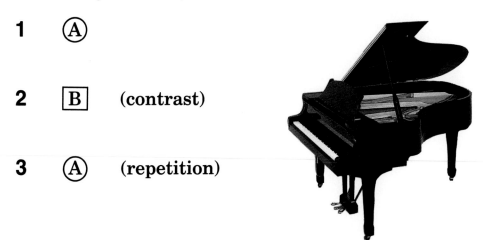

THE SOUND OF VOICES

Follow the words of the poem *The Wind* as you listen to the recording. Do you hear one voice? Several voices?

The Wind

I saw you toss the kites on high
And blow the birds about the sky;
And all around I heard you pass,
Like ladies' skirts across the grass—
   O wind, a-blowing all day long,
   O wind, that sings so loud a song!

I saw the different things you did,
But always you yourself you hid.
I felt you push, I heard you call,
I could not see yourself at all—
   O wind, a-blowing all day long,
   O wind, that sings so loud a song!

O you that are so strong and cold,
O blower, are you young or old?
Are you a beast of field and tree,
Or just a stronger child than me?
   O wind, a-blowing all day long,
   O wind, that sings so loud a song!

Robert Louis Stevenson

ONE VOICE–MANY VOICES

Listen for the solo parts in the recording of "Don't
Stay Away." Sing along on the chorus parts when
you can.

Don't Stay Away

African-American Spiritual

Chorus

My Lord says there's room e - nough, —

Room e - nough in the heav - en for us all.

My Lord says there's room e - nough, — So don't — stay a - way.

1. Oh, broth - er, Don't stay a - way, — Oh, broth - er, Don't stay a - way, —
2. Oh, sis - ter, Oh, sis - ter,

Oh, broth - er, Don't stay a - way, — Don't stay a - way.
Oh, sis - ter,

When you know the melody of "Don't Stay Away," try
singing the solo parts. The class will sing the chorus parts.

A SPECIAL SOUND

Your voice has a special sound (tone color) whether you use it to whisper, speak, shout, or sing. No one else has a voice that sounds exactly like yours.

Listen for the voices on the recording of "Polly Wolly Doodle." Can you tell who is singing?

Polly Wolly Doodle

American Folk Song

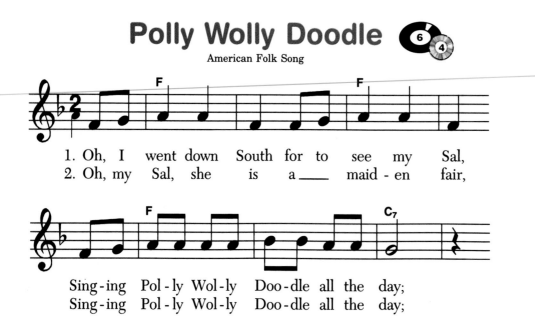

1. Oh, I went down South for to see my Sal,
2. Oh, my Sal, she is a ___ maid - en fair,

Sing - ing Pol - ly Wol - ly Doo - dle all the day;
Sing - ing Pol - ly Wol - ly Doo - dle all the day;

My — Sal, she is a — spunk-y gal,
With — curl-y eyes and — laugh-ing hair,

Sing-ing Pol-ly Wol-ly Doo-dle all the day.
Sing-ing Pol-ly Wol-ly Doo-dle all the day.

REFRAIN

Fare thee well, — fare thee well, — Fare thee well my fair-y fay, —

For I'm goin' to Loui-si - an - a, For to see my Su - sy - an - na,

Sing-ing Pol-ly Wol-ly Doo-dle all the day. ——

3. The partridge is a pretty bird,
   It has a speckled breast,
   It steals away the farmer's grain,
   And totes it to its nest! *Refrain*

4. The raccoon's tail is ringed around,
   The 'possum's tail is bare,
   The rabbit's got no tail at all,
   Just a little bitty bunch of hair! *Refrain*

THE SOUNDS OF INSTRUMENTS

Long ago, before Columbus discovered America,
people in Europe were listening to music played
on recorders.

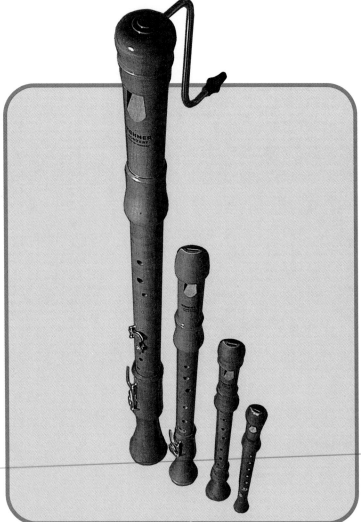

Listen to the sound of recorders in this music. Can
you hear the instrument that plays the lowest tones
and the one that plays the very highest melody?

Villancico . . . . Encina

Do you recognize any of the instruments on this page? Which instrument do you think plays the lowest tones? Listening to this recording may help you decide.

LISTENING LIBRARY 6 4 *The Special Sounds of Instruments*

The instruments pictured on this page are called *wind instruments.* Can you tell why?

The music in this recording is played by a group of wind instruments.

Scherzo . . . . .Bozza

BALLET MUSIC

Nutcracker Suite by Tchaikovsky is music written for a ballet, a kind of dance that often tells a story.

One of the pieces Tchaikovsky used in this ballet music is called "Dance of the Reed Flutes." Can you guess what instrument you will hear first?

"Dance of the Reed Flutes" from
Nutcracker Suite . . . . Tchaikovsky

● Melodies for Flute and Trumpet

Three flutes play the first melody.

A trumpet plays a contrasting melody.

Peter Illitch Tchaikovsky
(1840–1893)

Meet the Composer

Peter Illitch Tchaikovsky was born in Votkinsk, a little village in eastern Russia. From his earliest childhood Peter's main interest was music. But there were no concerts in Votkinsk, so most of Peter's music came from a music box that his father had brought from St. Petersburg. Peter would sit for hours listening to its tunes. As soon as he was big enough to sit at the piano, he began to make up tunes of his own.

Tchaikovsky composed a great deal of music. Today his beautiful melodies are heard in concert halls all over the world.

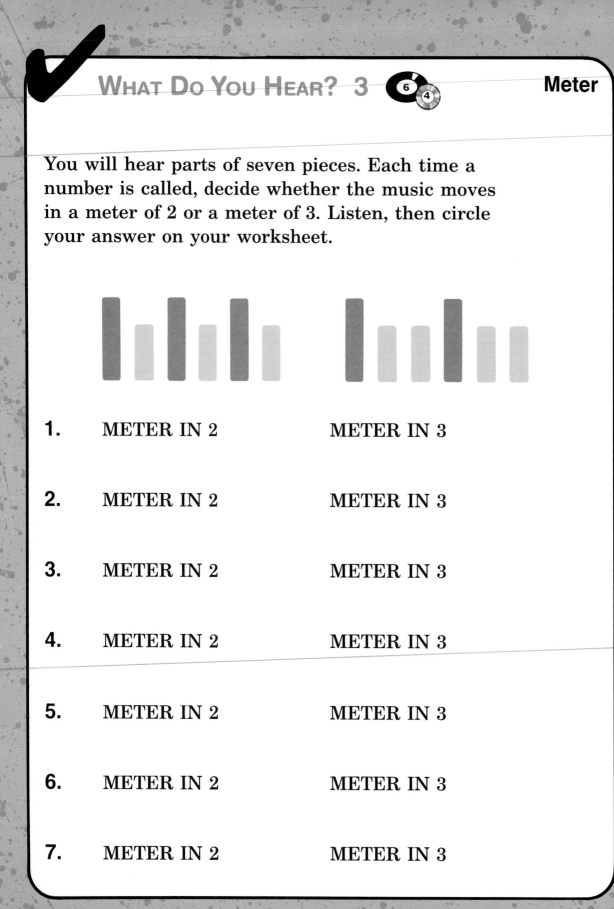

You will hear parts of seven pieces. Each time a number is called, decide whether the music moves in a meter of 2 or a meter of 3. Listen, then circle your answer on your worksheet.

1.   METER IN 2   METER IN 3

2.   METER IN 2   METER IN 3

3.   METER IN 2   METER IN 3

4.   METER IN 2   METER IN 3

5.   METER IN 2   METER IN 3

6.   METER IN 2   METER IN 3

7.   METER IN 2   METER IN 3

Look in the right-hand column for the line of notes
that matches the pattern of long and short lines in
the left-hand column. On your worksheet, write its
letter in the blank.

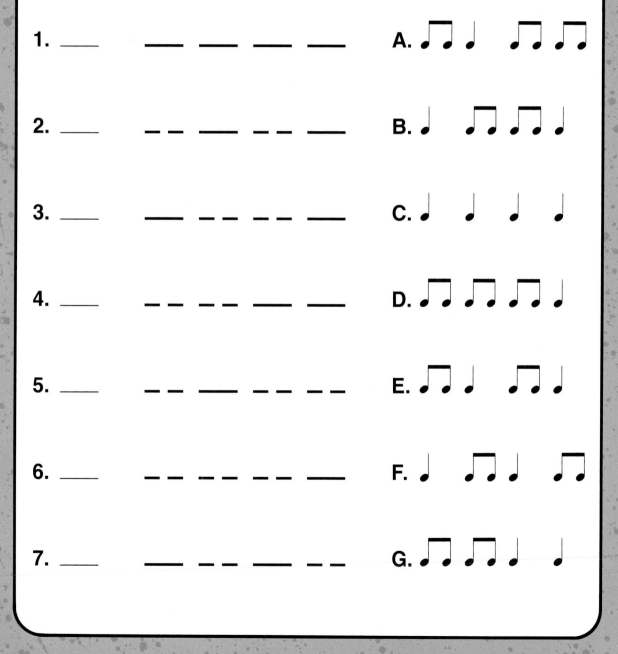

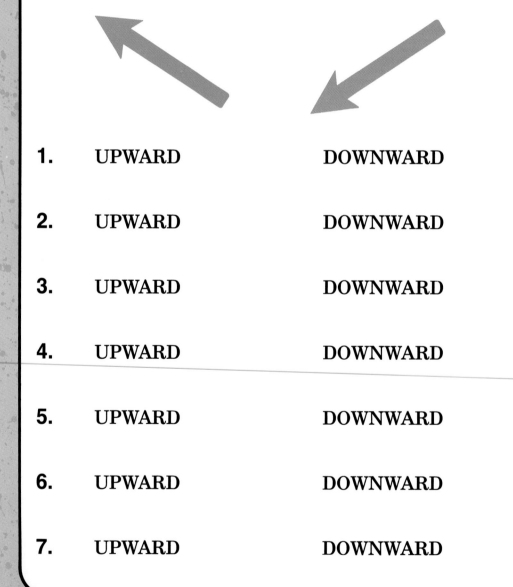

You will hear seven melodies. Listen carefully for the ending of each melody. If the tones move upward at the end of the melody, circle the word UPWARD on your worksheet. If the tones move downward, circle the word DOWNWARD.

1. UPWARD   DOWNWARD

2. UPWARD   DOWNWARD

3. UPWARD   DOWNWARD

4. UPWARD   DOWNWARD

5. UPWARD   DOWNWARD

6. UPWARD   DOWNWARD

7. UPWARD   DOWNWARD

TEST 4

Look at each example. If the notes repeat, write R in the blank. If they move by step, write S in the blank. If they leap, write L in the blank.

1. ___

2. ___

3. ___

4. ___

5. ___

6. ___

7. ___

8. ___

You will hear seven melodies. Each time a number is called, decide whether the tones in the melody move mostly by step, mostly by leap, or mostly by repeated tones. Listen, then circle your answer on your worksheet.

1.   STEP   LEAP   REPEAT

2.   STEP   LEAP   REPEAT

3.   STEP   LEAP   REPEAT

4.   STEP   LEAP   REPEAT

5.   STEP   LEAP   REPEAT

6.   STEP   LEAP   REPEAT

7.   STEP   LEAP   REPEAT

You will hear seven musical examples. Each example has two phrases. When a number is called, listen to both phrases. If the phrases are exactly alike, circle the word SAME on your worksheet. If the phrases are not alike, circle the word DIFFERENT. Listen, then circle your answer.

1.   SAME   DIFFERENT

2.   SAME   DIFFERENT

3.   SAME   DIFFERENT

4.   SAME   DIFFERENT

5.   SAME   DIFFERENT

6.   SAME   DIFFERENT

7.   SAME   DIFFERENT

Test 5

A. What is the form shown in each example below?

1. <u> A </u> <u>   </u>

2. <u> A </u> <u>   </u> <u>   </u>

3. <u> A </u> <u>   </u> <u>   </u>

4. <u> A </u> <u>   </u> <u>   </u>

B. The form of each song listed below is either AB or ABA. Look through the music and on your worksheet, write the name of the form in the blank.

1. The Dummy Line ____

2. Stodola Pumpa ____

3. I'd've Baked a Cake ____

4. Boil Them Cabbage Down ____

5. Nine Red Horsemen ____

6. Hand Me Down ____

You will hear six melodies. Each melody is played by a wind instrument. When a number is called, decide which instrument is playing. Listen, then circle your answer on your worksheet.

1.
recorder

trumpet

clarinet

trombone

flute

2.
recorder

trumpet

clarinet

trombone

flute

3.
recorder

trumpet

clarinet

trombone

flute

4.
recorder

trumpet

clarinet

trombone

flute

5.
recorder

trumpet

clarinet

trombone

flute

6.
recorder

trumpet

clarinet

trombone

flute

MAKING MUSIC

FRIENDS SING TOGETHER

One of the nicest things in life is having friends.
Friends who help each other are special.

Are you a special friend?

The Friendship Song

Words and Music by Philip Balsam and Dennis Lee

Re - mem - ber when _ now and then _ ev - 'ry - thing _ went wrong,

And then our friends _ would sing the friend - ship song, _____

You and I __ would near - ly cry _ to know their love _ was strong,

And by and by __ we'd start to sing _ a - long. _____

We'd sing, "Try a lit - tle long - er for your friend. _____

Try a lit - tle strong - er for your friend." _____

You work all night, — work all day, —

You just can't keep those wor-ried blues a-way. —————

Try a lit-tle long-er for your friend. ———

Try a lit-tle strong-er for your friend. ———

AN ADD-ON SONG

This is a special kind of song. To find out why, listen to the recording.

Green Leaves Grew All Around

Folk Song from England

1. All in ___ a ___ wood there grew a tree,
2. And on ___ this ___ tree there grew a limb,

The fin - est ___ tree you ev - er did see;
The fin - est ___ limb you ev - er did see;

The tree was in the wood,
The limb was on the tree,   The tree was in the wood,

And the green leaves grew all a - round, a-round, a-round,

And the green leaves grew all a - round.

Repeat for additional lines in verses 3–8.

3. And on this limb there was a branch,
    The finest branch you ever did see;
    The branch was on the limb,
    The limb was on the tree,
    The tree was in the wood,
    And the green leaves grew . . .

4. And on this branch there was a nest, . . .

5. And in this nest there was an egg, . . .

6. And in this egg there was a bird, . . .

7. And on this bird there was a wing, . . .

8. And on this wing there was a feather, . . .

KING OF THE CORNFIELD

Standing guard over a cornfield is a lonely job!

The Tired Scarecrow

Traditional

1. Stand - ing there, a tir - ed scare - crow,

Does - n't care how hard the wind blows,

Win - ter's chill is on the hill, and the

Scare - crow knows it's au - tumn. _____

2. He stood guard, king of the cornfield,
   Working hard, there in the cornfield,
   Did his best, now he can rest
   Till the planting time next year.

Bells

Dynamics—Soft or Loud

Listen to the recording of "Little Boy of the Sheep."
Then point to the word at the top of the page that
describes how the song is sung.

Little Boy of the Sheep

Folk Song from the Hebrides Islands   English Words by Alice Firgau

Sing me a song, pipe me a tune,

Guard the sheep well, O shep-herd boy.

Keep-ing the sheep all day, watch-ing they do not stray,

O - ver the hill - side, O shep - herd boy.

From FOLKSONGS AND FOLKLORE OF THE SOUTH UIST, by J. L. Campbell. © 1955 by Routledge & Kegan Paul, Ltd.

Listen for the instrument that pipes a tune
in this music.

Siciliana . . . . Bach

A Story with Music

This song is about a drummer boy. To find out what happens to him, follow the words as you listen to the recording.

Three Drummer Boys

French Folk Song   English Version by Margaret Marks

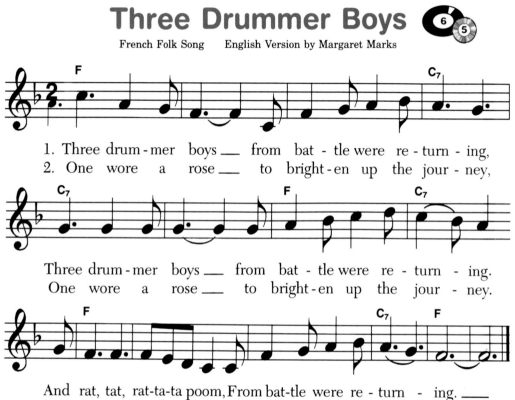

1. Three drum-mer boys __ from bat - tle were re - turn - ing,
2. One wore a rose __ to bright-en up the jour - ney,

Three drum-mer boys __ from bat - tle were re - turn - ing.
One wore a rose __ to bright-en up the jour - ney.

And rat, tat, rat-ta-ta poom, From bat-tle were re - turn - ing. __
And rat, tat, rat-ta-ta poom, To bright-en up the jour - ney. __

3.   Princess Marie was watching from her tower,

4.   "Sweet drummer boy, will you give me your flower?"

5.   "Give me your heart and give it to no other,"

6.   "Sweet drummer boy, you'll have to ask my father,"

7.   "O gracious King, will you give me your daughter?"

8.   "No drummer boy, you have no gold to court her,"

9.   "Three ships have I a-sailing on the water,"

10. "One's filled with gold, the other filled with treasure,"

11. "As for the third, I keep it for my pleasure,"

12. "Sweet drummer boy, then you may wed my daughter,"

13. "O gracious King, I wish to thank you kindly,"

14. "But in my land, we do not wed so blindly,"

● Drummer-Boy Band

Which part will you play in the Drummer-Boy Band?

THE FIREBIRD

The story that Igor Stravinsky tells in his ballet *The Firebird* is about the adventures of Prince Ivan, hero of many Russian folktales, and a mysterious bird with flaming feathers. In one part of the story, the firebird lulls a beautiful princess into a magic sleep to protect her from an evil king. Here is the music from that part of the story.

"Berceuse" from *Firebird Suite* .. Stravinsky

Ostinato Pattern

Here is a little pattern that you hear all through the music.

Listen for this sleepy bassoon melody near the beginning of the piece.

Igor Stravinsky
(1882–1971)

Meet the Composer

Igor Stravinsky was born in Russia. His father was a famous singer at the Russian Imperial Opera. Igor often went to opera rehearsals with his father and learned to love the musical theater when he was still a young boy.

During his lifetime Stravinsky composed many pieces for the musical theater. In addition to *The Firebird*, he wrote a ballet about a puppet called *Petrouchka* and another called *The Soldier's Tale*.

A Cradle Song

How would you sing a lullaby? Which list of words describes how a lullaby should be sung?

soft	jerky
quiet	fast
gentle	loud

Now Sleep, Little Fellow
(Dormite, niñito)

Folk Song from El Salvador

Now sleep, lit-tle fel - low,
Dor-mi - te, ni - ñi - to,

Sleep safe in your cra - dle;
No llo - res, chi - qui - to,

The shad - ows of ev - 'ning
Ven-drán an-ge - li - tos,

Creep o - ver the gar - den,
Las som-bras de no - che,

The rays of the moon - light,
Ray - i - tos de pla - ta,

Like fine threads of sil - ver,
Ray - i - tos de pla - ta,

Will shine on the ba - by
A - lum-bran a mi ni - ño,

A - sleep in his cra - dle.
Que es - ta en la cu - na.

The morn-ing will come soon
Ray - i - tos del sol, ___

With blue sky and sun - shine,
El cie - lo a - zul ___

The birds will a - wak - en
De - jan de dor - mir ___

To sing their sweet song.
Y em - pie - zan a vi - vir,

So sleep, lit - tle fel - low,
Dor - mi - te, ni - ñi - to,

While stars in the dark skies
Con o - jus de dia - man - tes,

Are twink - ling a - bove you
Es - tre - llas bri - llan - tes,

like flow - ers of heav - en.
Flo - ri - do el cie - lo.

FOLLOW THE PHRASE LINES

Follow the phrase lines marked over the music as you listen to "Garden Song." Are all the phrases the same length? Are some of the phrases short and others long?

Garden Song

Words and Music by David Mallett

1. Inch by inch, row by row, —
2. Pull - in' weeds and pick - in' stones, —

Gon - na make this gar - den grow, —
Man is made of dreams and bones, —

All it takes is a rake and a hoe
Feel the need to — grow my — own

and   a   piece of fer - tile   ground. ___
'cause the time is close at   hand. _____

Inch   by   inch,   row by   row, _
Grain for   grain,   sun and   rain _

Some - one bless the   seeds I   sow,
Find   my   way   in   na - ture's chain,

Some - one warm them   from   be - low _
Tune   my   bod - y   and   my   brain _

'til   the   rain comes tum - bl - ing   down.
to   the   mu - sic   from _ the   land.

3. Plant your rows straight and long,
    Temper them with prayer and song,
    Mother Earth will make you strong
    if you give her love and care.
    Old crow watching hungrily
    From his perch in yonder tree,
    In my garden I'm as free
    as that feathered thief up there.

MELODY AND COUNTERMELODY

Trace the rise and fall of this melody in the air. Pretend you are painting an autumn scene with a big paintbrush.

Autumn

English Folk Song

1. Au - tumn comes, the sum - mer is past,
2. Au - tumn comes, but let us be glad,

Win - ter will come too soon. _____
Sing - ing an au - tumn tune. _____

Stars will shine clear - er, skies seem near - er,
Hearts will be light - er, nights be bright - er,

Un - der the Har - vest Moon. _____
Un - der the Har - vest Moon. _____

Bells

Autumn's Countermelody

Countermelody

1. Au - tumn comes, the sum - mer is past,
2. Au - tumn comes, but let us be glad,

Win - ter will come too soon.
Sing - ing an au - tumn tune.

Stars will shine clear - er, skies seem near - er,
Hearts will be light - er, nights be bright - er,

Un - der the Har - vest Moon.
Un - der the Har - vest Moon.

Autumn Woods

I like the woods
    In autumn
When dry leaves hide the ground,
When the trees are bare
And the wind sweeps by
With a lonesome rushing sound.

I can rustle the leaves
    In autumn
And I can make a bed
In the thick dry leaves
That have fallen
From the bare trees
Overhead.

James S. Tippett

SINGING A STORY

A song that tells a story is called a *ballad*. Read the words of this ballad. What kind of story does it tell?

A Little Ship

French Folk Song   English Version by Margaret Marks

1. A lit - tle ship once went a - sail - ing,

A lit - tle ship once went a - sail - ing,

But on the o - o - o-cean lost its way,

But on the o - o - o-cean lost its way, *O-hé, o - hé!*

2. And after weeks and weeks of sailing *(2 times)*
   There were no ra-ra-rations left one day. *(2 times)*
   Ohé, ohé!

3. The crew drew lots to choose the sailor
   Whom they should ea-ea-eat for *déjeuner.*

4. The choice fell on the youngest sailor,
   He was the one, one, one they would *sauté.*

5. And while they argued how to serve him,
   With lemon sau-sau-sauce or *Bordelaise,*

6. A hundred thousand flying fishes
   Jumped on the de-de-deck and there they lay.

7. And so the sailors ate the fishes.
   The boy was sa-sa-saved, oh happy day!

8. If you've enjoyed this little ditty
   We'll sing it o-o-over right away.

● A Part for Bells

Play this part to accompany "A Little Ship." You will
need two bells—the G bell and the D bell.

FLOWER SONG FROM CHINA

Play a sound on a ringing instrument for each X.

The Jasmine Flower

Folk Song from China   English Words Adapted by Julia Bingham

1. See __ this branch __ of __ sweet - est __ flow'rs,
2. Take __ this branch __ of __ jas - mine __ flow'rs,

Plucked __ at morn __ from __ dew - y ___ bow'rs;
Plucked __ at morn __ from __ dew - y ___ bow'rs;

Sent with love ___ to greet me,
Given with love ___ to greet you,

Breath - ing friend - ship sweet.
Breath - ing friend - ship sweet.

● Add a Part

R.H.

L.H.

MAKE A WISH

What would you like to find
at the end of a rainbow?

Look to the Rainbow

from *Finian's Rainbow*

Words by E. Y. Harburg   Music by Burton Lane

Look,   look,   look   to   the   rain - bow.

Fol - low it   o - ver the   hill ___ and   stream.

Look,   look,   look   to   the   rain - bow.

Fol - low the   fel - low   who   fol - lows   a   dream.

Fol - low the   fel - low,   Fol - low the   fel - low,

Fol - low the   fel - low who   fol - lows   a   dream.

A Song for All Seasons

You can sing this beautiful song at any time of the year.

May Day Carol

English Folk Song

Gently

1. The moon shines bright, The stars give light,
2. A branch of May I bring to you

A lit - tle be - fore 'tis day.
As at ___ the door I stand.

Our Heav - en - ly Fa - ther, He called to us
'Tis but ___ a sprout well ___ bud - ded out,

And bid us to wake and pray.
The work of ___ our Lord's hands.

A - wake, a - wake, O pret - ty, pret - ty maid,
My song is done, I must ___ be ___ gone,

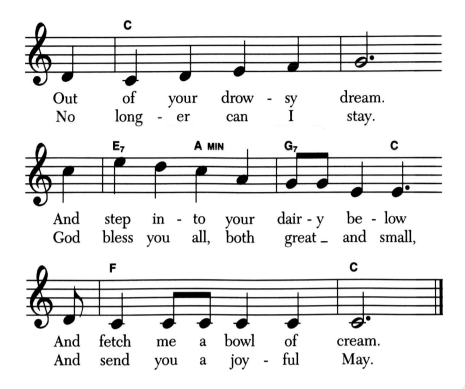

C

Out of your drow - sy dream.
No long - er can I stay.

E₇   **A MIN**   **G₇**   **C**

And step in - to your dair - y be - low
God bless you all, both great _ and small,

F   **C**

And fetch me a bowl of cream.
And send you a joy - ful May.

There Is But One May

There is but one May in the year,
  And sometimes May is wet and cold;
There is but one May in the year
  Before the year grows old.

Yet though it be the chilliest May,
  With least of sun and most of showers,
Its wind and dew, its night and day,
  Bring up the flowers.

Christina Georgina Rossetti

A Musical Greeting

This song would be a good one to sing for United
Nations Day. Can you tell why?

We Come to Greet You in Peace
(Hevenu Shalom Aleichem)
Hebrew Folk Song

Play a tambourine accompaniment
all through the song.

SONG WITHOUT WORDS

Some songs have no words—only syllables like *tra la la.* The *bims, boms,* and *biris* in this song are fun to sing. Sing along with the recording when you can.

Bim Bom

Jewish Folk Song

Bim bom, bi - ri bi - ri bom

Bi - ri bi - ri bom bom bi - ri bi - ri bim bom

Bim bom bom, bi - ri bim bom bom, bi - ri

bim bom bi - ri, bi - ri bim bom bom,

Bim bom bom, bi - ri bim bom bom, bi - ri

bim bom bi - ri, bi - ri bim bom bom.

MUSIC FOR HARPSICHORD

The instrument shown in the picture
above is called a *harpsichord*. You will find a picture
of one of the harpsichord's relatives on page 100
in your music book. Look at the pictures of the two
instruments. Can you see that the harpsichord
and the piano are related?

Here is some harpsichord music by Handel. Can you
hear that the sound of the harpsichord is different
from the sound of the piano?

The Harmonious Blacksmith . . . . Handel

Here is the melody, or theme, that you hear at the beginning of *The Harmonious Blacksmith*. You might try following the music as you listen to the recording again.

George Frideric Handel
(1685–1759)

Meet the Composer

George Frideric Handel was born in the small German village of Halle. When he was still a child, George decided that he would be a musician when he grew up.

Handel went on to become one of the greatest composers of all times. During his lifetime he wrote music to be sung and music for all kinds of instruments, including the well-known harpsichord piece *The Harmonious Blacksmith*.

Read the sentences below. On your worksheet, write T in the blank if the sentence is true. Write F in the blank if the sentence is false.

1. Recognizing like phrases makes a song easier to learn. _____

2. An ostinato is a pattern that is repeated over and over again. _____

3. All songs should be sung at the same tempo. _____

4. Cymbals and drums are good instruments to use with a marching song. _____

5. The words of a song often give a clue as to how the song should be sung. _____

6. A lullaby should be sung loud and fast. _____

7. A ballad is a song that tells a story. _____

8. The term *dynamics* means the loudness and softness of sound. _____

9. A coda comes at the end of a piece. _____

10. This is a repeat sign— :‖ . _____

You will hear four sets of pieces. In each set, one piece is in a slow tempo, the other in a fast tempo. Listen to both pieces, decide which is slow and which is fast, then circle your answer on your worksheet.

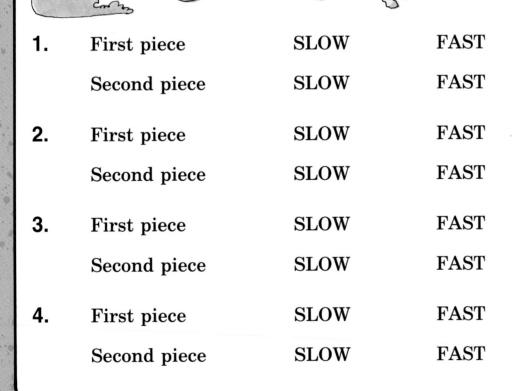

1.   First piece   SLOW   FAST

        Second piece   SLOW   FAST

2.   First piece   SLOW   FAST

        Second piece   SLOW   FAST

3.   First piece   SLOW   FAST

        Second piece   SLOW   FAST

4.   First piece   SLOW   FAST

        Second piece   SLOW   FAST

"LET'S COMMUNICATE"
A Theme Musical by Carmino Ravosa

Please Enter

Guide 1: Welcome to The (name) Museum of Communication and to our show, "Let's Communicate." Members of Miss (name) class will be your guides.

Step Right This Way

Words and Music by Carmino Ravosa

1.–3. Step right this way. __ Step right this way. __ The

Last time to Coda

tour is start-ing, _ so step right this way. _ Step right this way. __

1. Keep to - geth - er and pay at - ten - tion and
2. No push - ing and no rush - ing and
3. You'll en - joy ___ ev - 'ry min - ute of ___ it, yes

step live - ly, oh did I men - tion to
no talk - ing, and no touch - ing, so
we know _ that you're gon - na love _ it, so

Coda

Step right this way!

Guide 2: What is communication?

Guide 3: Communication is an exchange of feelings, thoughts, or information.

Guide 4: When you talk with someone, you are communicating with spoken words. When you write a letter, you are communicating with written words.

Guide 5: People are the only creatures on earth who can express thoughts in words.

Guide 6: Some scientists think that people began to speak about 34,000 years ago. And before people began to talk, they probably used gestures to communicate.

Guide 7: We still use gestures. When we shake hands, we are saying "Hello" without making a sound.

Guide 8: In China, people bow. Laplanders rub noses. Latin American men embrace. Soldiers salute.

Guide 9: And clowns! They always talk without saying a word.

He's a Clown

Words and Music by Carmino Ravosa

He's a clown, he's a clown, he's a clown. He's the
clown, he's a clown, he's a clown. When he

fun - ni - est man in the town. From his
trips and he falls on the ground. He's not

head to his toe, we all know, He's a clown. _____ He's a
play - ing a part, in his heart, He's a

clown. He'd rath - er be a clown than the Pres - i - dent.

He'd rath - er be a clown than a king. He'd

rath-er be a clown than an as-tro-naut, Or an-y oth-er thing.

He's a clown, he's a clown, he's a clown. Seems he

does ev-'ry-thing up-side down, He's not play-ing a part, in his heart,

to Coda C *D.S. Coda* G₇ *(clown)* C *(Chorus)*

He's a clown.___ He's a clown, he's a clown. I'm a clown! He's a clown!

Guide 10: There are many ways to communicate. Signs communicate: No Smoking, Deer Crossing, Watch Out for Children.

Guide 11: And how about *sound* as a way of communicating? We have fire alarms and police whistles—even doorbells.

Guide 12: People talk about how great it would be if there was a language that everyone in the world could understand. Well, in a way, we have such a language—music! But you have to sing it or play it.

Music Is Not Music Unless You Sing It

Words and Music by Carmino Ravosa

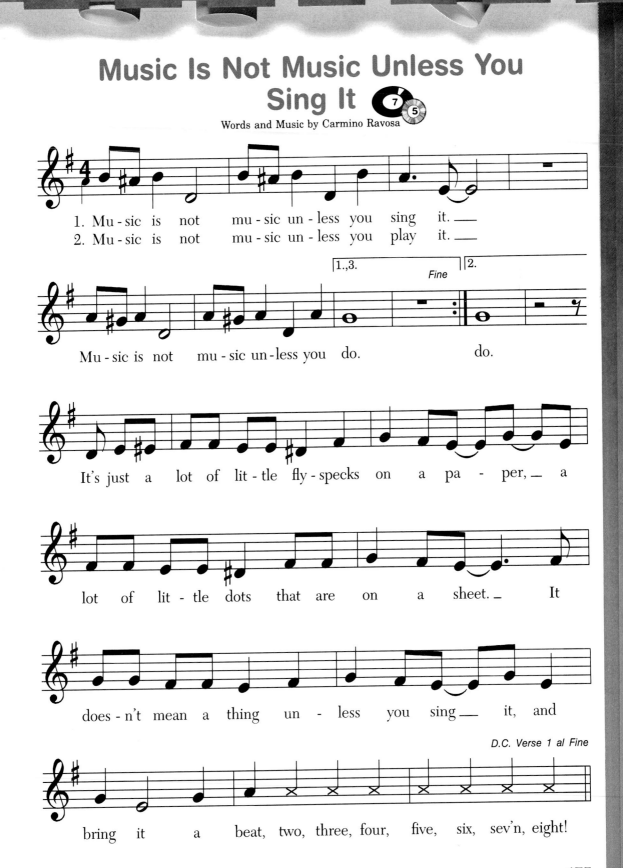

Extra, Extra

Words and Music by Carmino Ravosa

Ex - tra, ex - tra, read ___ all ___ a - bout it,

Ex - tra, ex - tra, read ___ all ___ a - bout it,

Ex - tra, ex - tra, read ___ all _ a - bout it, here. ___ here. ___

If there's a nick - el _____ that you've got, ___
Guess what ___ mov - ie _____ star got wed? ___

get the news, ___ while it's hot. ___
Did you hear ___ what the Pres - i - dent said? ___

Ex - tra, ex - tra, read ___ all _ a - bout it here. _____

Guide 14: Thomas Edison had to try and try again before he got the phonograph to work.

If at First You Don't Succeed

Words and Music by Carmino Ravosa

If at first you don't suc-ceed, Try and try a - gain.

If at first you don't suc-ceed, Try and try a - gain,

And you will find, If you've got the mind,
And you will see, Take __ it from me.

To do it, go through it, you will.
Be - gin it, you'll win it, you'll see.

soft
If at first you don't suc-ceed, Try and try a - gain.

loud
If at first you don't suc-ceed, Try and try a - gain!

Guide 15: And to bring us right up to date, we have our favorite invention—the computer.

My Computer and Me

Words and Music by Carmino Ravosa

My com-put-er and me, My com-put-er and me,

We're as hap-py can be, My com-put-er and me.

We can add, sub-tract, or mul-ti-ply, di-vide, as you can see.
In play-ing games it does-n't cheat, get bored and want to go.

We can read or write or draw or paint or write a sym-pho-ny.
It doesn't get mad or jeal-ous like some-one that I know.

My com-put-er and me, My com-put-er and me.

Guide 16: We've come a long way in communications—or have we? A smile still communicates more than any word. Do you know that a smile is the shortest distance between two people?

The Shortest Distance Between Two People

Words and Music by Carmino Ravosa

The short-est dis - tance be - tween two peo - ple is a smile.

Fine

The short-est dis - tance be - tween two peo - ple is a smile.

The short-est dis - tance,   The path of least re - sist - ance,

D.C. al Fine

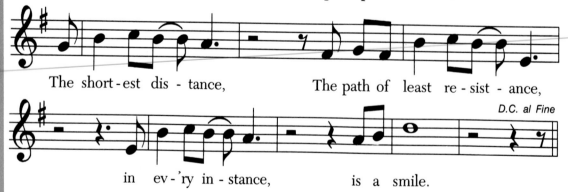

in   ev-'ry in - stance,   is   a   smile.

Guide 17: When was the last time you said "Thank you" to your mother or father or your teacher or your best friend—said "Thank you for being you"?

Thank You for Being You

Words and Music by Carmino Ravosa

Thank you for all the things _ that you've done for me;
Thank you for all the time — that you've spent with me;

All the things _ you've made fun for me.
All the things — that you've meant to me.

1.
Thank you for _ be-ing you.
Thank you for _ be-ing you.

2.
you.

Be-ing

you be-ing you be-ing you be-ing you.

Thank you for all the things _ that you've taught to me;

All the love _ that you've brought to me.

Thank you for _ be-ing you, Be-ing you, Be-ing you!

Guide 18: No matter how well we get along with someone near to us, we've got to get along with everybody else in the world.

Guide 19: So let's communicate. We've got to get together before it's too late.

Let's Communicate

Words and Music by Carmino Ravosa

Let's com - mun - i - cate, _ let's com - mun - i - cate. _ We've

got to get to - geth - er be - fore it's too late. _ Let's com -

mun - i - cate, _ Let's com - mun - i - cate, _ We've

got to get to - geth - er and we just can't wait. _

We should try to get a - long with each oth - er, We've

got to try to un-der-stand one an-oth-er.

Coda

Let's com-mun-i - cate, _ Let's com-mun-i - cate, _ We've

slower

got to get to-geth-er and we just can't wait. _

Jan	1 2 3 4 5 6
	7 8 9 10 11 12 13 14 15
	16 17 18 19 20 21 22 23 24
	25 26 27 28 29 30 31

Feb	1 2 3 4 5 6
	7 8 9 10 11 12 13 14 15
	16 17 18 19 20 21 22 23 24
	25 26 27 28

Mar	1 2 3 4 5 6
	7 8 9 10 11 12 13 14 15
	16 17 18 19 20 21 22 23 24
	25 26 27 28 29 30 31

Apr	1 2 3 4 5 6
	7 8 9 10 11 12 13 14 15
	16 17 18 19 20 21 22 23 24
	25 26 27 28 29 30

May	1 2 3 4 5 6
	7 8 9 10 11 12 13 14 15
	16 17 18 19 20 21 22 23 24
	25 26 27 28 29 30 31

Jun	1 2 3 4 5 6
	7 8 9 10 11 12 13 14 15
	16 17 18 19 20 21 22 23 24
	25 26 27 28 29 30

Jul	1 2 3 4 5 6
	7 8 9 10 11 12 13 14 15
	16 17 18 19 20 21 22 23 24
	25 26 27 28 29 30 31

Aug	1 2 3 4 5 6
	7 8 9 10 11 12 13 14 15
	16 17 18 19 20 21 22 23 24
	25 26 27 28 29 30 31

Sep	1 2 3 4 5 6
	7 8 9 10 11 12 13 14 15
	16 17 18 19 20 21 22 23 24
	25 26 27 28 29 30

Oct	1 2 3 4 5 6
	7 8 9 10 11 12 13 14 15
	16 17 18 19 20 21 22 23 24
	25 26 27 28 29 30 31

Nov	1 2 3 4 5 6
	7 8 9 10 11 12 13 14 15
	16 17 18 19 20 21 22 23 24
	25 26 27 28 29 30

Dec	1 2 3 4 5 6
	7 8 9 10 11 12 13 14 15
	16 17 18 19 20 21 22 23 24
	25 26 27 28 29 30 31

OUR NATIONAL ANTHEM

What should you do when our national anthem is sung or played?

The Star-Spangled Banner

Words by Francis Scott Key   Music by John Stafford Smith

Oh, — say! can you see, by the dawn's ear - ly light,

What so proud - ly we hailed at the twi-light's last gleam - ing,

Whose broad stripes and bright stars, through the per - il - ous fight,

O'er the ram - parts we watched were so gal - lant - ly stream - ing?

And the rock - ets' red glare, the bombs burst - ing in air,

Gave proof through the night that our flag was still there.

Oh, say, does that _ Star-Span-gled Ban - ner _ yet _ wave _

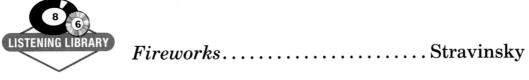

O'er the land __ of the free and the home of the brave.

National holidays are often celebrated with fireworks. Listen for the "fireworks" in this piece. What makes the music so exciting?

Fireworks. .Stravinsky

Here is how a poet describes fireworks.

Fireworks

They rise like sudden fiery flowers
    That burst upon the night,
Then fall to earth in burning showers
    Of crimson, blue, and white.

Like buds too wonderful to name,
    Each miracle unfolds,
And catherine-wheels begin to flame
    Like whirling marigolds.

Rockets and roman candles make
    An orchard of the sky,
Whence magic trees their petals shake
    Upon each gazing eye.

James Reeves

LET FREEDOM RING

What do you think of when you read the words
liberty and *freedom*? Think about those words when
you sing this song.

America

Traditional Melody   Words by Samuel Francis Smith

My coun-try! 'tis   of thee, Sweet land of   lib - er - ty,

Of thee I   sing;   Land where my   fa - thers died,

Land of the   Pil - grims' pride, From ev - 'ry __ moun - tain - side

Let __ free - dom   ring!

Our fathers' God, to Thee, Author of liberty,
To Thee we sing; Long may our land be bright
With freedom's holy light; Protect us by Thy might,
Great God, our King!

FROM SEA TO SHINING SEA

Some of the words in this song paint a picture of our land. Can you paint a picture that would show America, the beautiful?

America, the Beautiful

Words by Katharine Lee Bates   Music by Samuel A. Ward

1. O beau-ti-ful for spa-cious skies, For am-ber waves of grain,
2. O beau-ti-ful for pa-triot dream That sees be-yond the years

For pur-ple moun-tain maj-es-ties A-bove the fruit-ed plain!
Thine al-a-bas-ter cit-ies gleam, Un-dimmed by hu-man tears!

A-mer-i-ca! A-mer-i-ca! God shed His grace on thee,

And crown thy good with broth-er-hood From sea to shin-ing sea!

AN OLD FAVORITE

"Yankee Doodle" is a favorite song of boys and girls all over America. Many verses have been written for the tune. Here are the words that you may know best.

Yankee Doodle came to town
Riding on a pony,
Stuck a feather in his cap
And called it macaroni.

Yankee Doodle

Traditional   Words by Dr. Richard Shuckburgh

1. 𝄽 Fath'r and I went down to camp,
2. And there we saw a thou-sand men,

A - long with Cap - tain Good - in',
As rich as Squire____ Da - vid;

And there we saw the men and boys
And what they wast - ed ev - 'ry day,

As thick as hast - y pud - din'.
I wish it could be sav - ed.

REFRAIN

Yan - kee Doo - dle, keep it up, Yan - kee Doo - dle dan - dy,

Mind the mu - sic and the step And with the girls be hand - y.

3. And there was Captain Washington
Upon a slapping stallion,
A-giving orders to his men;
I guess there was a million.

● Parts for Percussion

Which percussion part will you play? Which instrument
will you use to accompany this marching song?

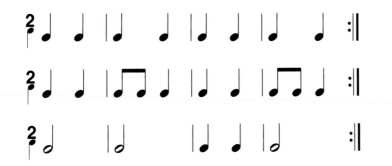

SOUND OF HALLOWEEN

Listen for the Halloween sounds that accompany the voices on the recording of "The Ghost of John."

The Ghost of John

Words and Music by Martha Grubb

Have you seen the ghost of John?

Long white bones with the skin all gone, _____

Oo, Oo, _____

Would-n't it be chil-ly with no skin on!

Play your own accompaniment for "The Ghost of John." Which pattern will you choose?

Bells

Play 4 times.

Guiro

Play 4 times.

HALLOWEEN NIGHT

Read the words of this song as a poem. Then think of
ways to use your singing voice to make the song exciting.

Hallowe'en

Words by Harry Behn   Music by Milton Kaye

To - night is the night when dead leaves fly

Like witch - es on switch - es a - cross the sky.

When elf and sprite flit through the night on a

moon - y sheen, It's Hal - low - e'en.

Try this accompaniment for guiro and voices.
Then make up an accompaniment of your own.

Guiro

Voices

Oooh.   Oooh.

193

HALLOWEEN CAT

The first line of this song tells you that an old black cat hates Halloween. The last line tells you why.

My Old Black Cat Hates Halloween

Words and Music by Linda Williams

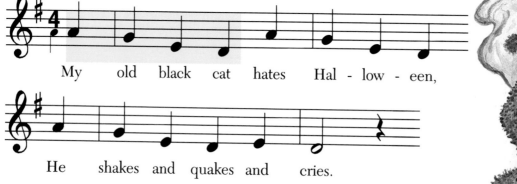

My old black cat hates Hal - low - een,

He shakes and quakes and cries.

He should be good on Hal - low - een,

But much to my sur - prise,

He stays in bed and hides his head,

Now, why does he do that?

© 1986 SUNDANCE MUSIC

"Me - ow," he says, "Me - ow," he says,

"I'm just a scare - dy cat!"

Halloween Indignation Meeting

A sulky witch
  and a surly cat
And a scowly owl
  and a skeleton sat
With a grouchy ghost
  and a waspish bat,
And angrily snarled
  and chewed the fat.

It seems they were
  all upset and riled
That they couldn't frighten
  the Modern Child,
Who was much too knowing
  and much too wild
And considered Hallowe'en
  spooks too mild.

Said the witch, "They call this
  the *human* race.
Yet the kiddies inhabit
  Outer Space;
They bob for comets,
  and eat ice cream
From flying saucers,
  to get up steam!"

"I'm a shade of my former self,"
  said the skeleton.
"I shiver and shake
  like so much gelatine,
Indeed I'm a pitiful
  sight to see—
I'm scareder of *kids*
  than they are of *me!*"

Margaret Fishback

HARVEST HOME

Come, Ye Thankful People, Come

Words by Henry Alford   Music by George J. Elvey

1. Come, ye thank-ful peo-ple, come, Raise the song of har-vest home;
2. All the bless-ings of the field, All the stores the gar-dens yield;

All is safe-ly gath-ered in, Ere the win-ter storms be-gin;
All the fruits in full sup-ply, Rip-ened 'neath the sum-mer sky;

God, our Mak-er, doth pro-vide For our wants to be sup-plied;
All that Spring with boun-teous hand Scat-ters o'er the smil-ing land;

Come to God's own tem-ple, come, Raise the song of har-vest home.
All that lib-'ral au-tumn pours From her rich o'er-flow-ing stores.

Bells or recorder

A HYMN OF PRAISE

Listen to the recording of this song. Can you name the instrument that accompanies the voices?

For the Beauty of the Earth

Words by Folliott S. Pierpoint   Music Arranged from Conrad Kocher

1. For the _ beau - ty of the earth,

For the beau - ty of the skies,

For the _ love which from our birth

O - ver and a - round us lies,

Lord of all, to Thee we raise

This our hymn of grate - ful praise.

2. For the beauty of each hour
   Of the day and of the night,
   Hill and vale and tree and flower,
   Sun and moon and stars of light, . . .

SWAHILI PRAYER

'Sante-sana

Words and Music by Linda Williams

1. 'San - te - sa - na, — Lord, for the morn - ing, —
2. 'San - te - sa - na, — Lord, for the hunt - ers, —

'San - te - sa - na, — Lord, for the light,
'San - te - sa - na, — Lord, for their might,

For the bird that sings, For the joy it brings;
Guide them as they roam, Bring them safe - ly home,

'San - te - sa - na, — Thank you Lord.
'San - te - sa - na, — Thank you Lord.

3. For the cattle safe from the lion,
   For the village safe in your sight,
   For the fields of grain,
   Blessed with sun and rain,
   'Sante-sana, Thank you Lord.

4. Bless my brothers, Lord, and my sisters,
   Bless our slumber, Lord, through the night,
   Bring another day,
   Hear us when we pray,
   'Sante-sana, Thank you Lord.

A SONG FOR WINTER

In some parts of our country, wintertime is snow time.
What kind of things do you do out of doors in wintertime?

Winter Wonderland

Words by Dick Smith   Music by Felix Bernard

Sleigh-bells ring,   are you lis-t'nin'?
Gone a-way   is the blue-bird

In the lane   snow is glis-t'nin',
Here to stay   is a new bird,

A beau-ti-ful sight, __ We're hap-py to-night, __
He's sing-ing a song __ as we go a-long, __

1.

2.

Walk-in' in a win-ter won-der land!   land!

In the mead-ow we can build a snow-man,

And pre-tend that he's a cir-cus clown;

We'll have lots of fun with Mis-ter Snow-man

Un - til the oth-er kid-dies knock 'im down!

When it snows, ain't it thrill-in'?

Tho' your nose gets a chill-in',

We'll frol-ic and play _ the Es-ki-mo way, _

Walk-in' in a win-ter won-der land!

SPIN THE DREYDL

Some children celebrate Chanukah with games and songs. The game Spin the Dreydl, though hundreds of years old, is still popular today.

Listen for the tambourine pattern in the recording of this song. Then find the pattern in the color box.

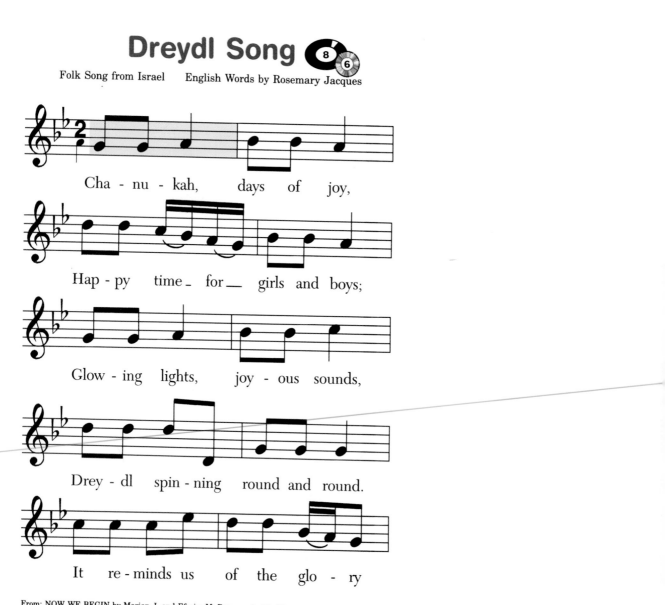

Dreydl Song

Folk Song from Israel   English Words by Rosemary Jacques

Cha - nu - kah,   days   of   joy,

Hap - py   time _ for _ girls   and   boys;

Glow - ing   lights,   joy - ous   sounds,

Drey - dl   spin - ning   round and   round.

It   re - minds us   of   the   glo - ry

From: NOW WE BEGIN by Marian J. and Efraim M. Rosenzweig. Used by permission of Union of American Hebrew Congregations.

Of the days of Ju - dah Mac-ca-bee;

Spin the drey - dl, tell the sto - ry

Oh, what fun for you and me.

FESTIVAL OF LIGHT

Show that you hear the two sections of this song. Tap the steady beat during section A. Clap the steady beat during section B.

Make a Little Music for Chanukah

Words and Music by David Eddleman

A

1. When the chill is in the air and nights are get-ting long,
2. Now the can-dles all are burn-ing, burn-ing, oh, so bright,

Peo-ple light their can-dles and they sing a hap-py song
Fill-ing ev-'ry hap-py heart with warm and cheer-ful light,

A - bout a He-brew he - ro and a lan-tern burn-ing bright,
Tell-ing us that once there was a mir - a - cle, they say,

Then you know you must get read - y for the Fes-ti-val of Light.
When the lan-tern burned for eight long nights with oil for but one day.

Make a lit-tle mu-sic, make a lit-tle mu-sic,

Make a lit-tle mu-sic for Cha-nu-kah;

Make a lit-tle mu-sic, make a lit-tle mu-sic,

Make a lit-tle mu-sic for Cha-nu-kah.

● Patterns for Percussion

Play these patterns with section A.

Play these patterns with section B.

December

I like days
with a snow-white collar,
and nights when the moon
is a silver dollar,
and hills are filled
with eiderdown stuffing
and your breath makes smoke
like an engine puffing.

I like days
when feathers are snowing,
and all the eaves
have petticoats showing,
and the air is cold,
and the wires are humming,
but you feel all warm . . .
with Christmas coming!

Aileen Fisher

A SONG FOR CHRISTMAS

Follow along in your book as you listen to this merry Christmas song. Sing along when you can.

Merry, Merry Christmas

Traditional

Mer - ry, mer - ry Christ - mas ev - 'ry - where,

Cheer - i - ly it rings out through the air.

Christ - mas bells, Christ - mas trees, Christ - mas car - ols on the breeze.

Mer - ry, mer - ry Christ - mas ev - 'ry - where,

Cheer - i - ly it rings out on the air.

Why should we so joy - ous be, On this Christ - mas morn - ing?

An - gels sang in Beth - le - hem, On this Christ - mas morn - ing.

CHRISTMAS BELLS

I heard the bells on Christmas day
Their old familiar carols play,
And wild and sweet the words repeat
Of peace on earth, good will to men.

Christmas Is Coming

Polish Folk Tune   Words by Helen Bonney Kilduff

1. Christ - mas is com - ing; Oh, the hap - py day!
2. Christ - mas bells ring - ing On the frost - y air,

Christ - mas is com - ing, Sing a roun - de - lay.
Glad voic - es sing - ing, Joy is ev - 'ry - where.

Through the air gay tunes are ring - ing: Can it be the
Peace on earth, good - will they're bring - ing, Let us come and

an - gels sing - ing On this hap - py day?
join the sing - ing; Christ - mas Day is here!

A Swedish Christmas Song

In Sweden, children sing this song as they dance around the Christmas tree.

Christmas Is Here Again

Swedish Folk Song

Christ-mas is here a-gain, Oh, Christ-mas is here a-gain,

Our hol-i-days will last till Eas-ter.

Then it is Eas-ter-time, Oh, then it is Eas-ter-time,

And Eas-ter joy will last till Christ-mas.

Words copyright 1934, 1961 G. Schirmer, Inc. Reprinted by permission.

Countermelody for Bells

CHRISTMAS SONG FROM MEXICO

To children in Mexico, Christmas Eve is an exciting time.

Piñata

Christmas Song from Mexico   English Words by Nona K. Duffy

Bril-liant lan-terns are light-ed, Our friends are in-vit-ed,

In cho-rus u-nit-ed, "¡Pi - ña - ta!"

There's no need to re-mind us, With blind-folds they'll bind us,

They'll turn and they'll wind us, "¡Pi - ña-ta!"

The *pi - ña - ta,* the *pi - ña - ta,*

Holds the can - dies for neigh - bors and cous - ins;

We will whack it, we will crack it,

And the good - ies will fall down in doz - ens.

All the chil - dren will scram - ble for can - dy,

All the chil - dren will scram - ble and shout;

All the chil - dren will grab for a cook - ie

And the oth - er good things that spill out.

A CHRISTMAS LULLABY

How do you think this song should be sung? The headline at the top of the page will give you a hint.

The Rocking Carol

Mexican Christmas Carol

A la ru - ru - ru, my ba - by dear - est,

Oh, sleep, my ba - by, oh, sleep, my fair - est. _____

The cat - tle now have ceased their gen - tle low - ing,

The si - lence of the beasts, de - vo - tion show - ing.

A la ru - ru - ru, my ba - by dear - est,

Oh, sleep, my ba - by, oh, sleep, my fair - est. _____

On this recording you will hear another Christmas lullaby played by brass instruments. If you know the tune, hum along.

LISTENING LIBRARY 9 6

Coventry Carol . . . . Old English Melody

Amedeo Modigliani, *Gypsy Woman with Baby* (detail). National Gallery of Art, Chester Dale Collection, Washington, D.C.

GYPSY WOMAN WITH BABY   *Amedeo Modigliani*

SING WITH JOY

Try not to get lost in this add-on song. Follow the words as you listen to the recording. Join in when you can.

Children, Go Where I Send Thee

American Folk Song

1. Chil-dren, go where I send thee; How shall I send thee?

I will send thee one by one. —

Well, one was the lit-tle bit-ty ba - by, —

Wrapped in swad-dling cloth - ing, —

Ly-ing in the man - ger. —

Born, born, _ oh, — Born in Beth - le - hem. ____

2. Children, go where I send thee;
   How shall I send thee?
   I will send thee two by two.
   Well, two was the Paul and Silas,
   One was the little bitty baby,
   Wrapped in swaddling clothing,
   Lying in the manger.
   Born, born, oh,
   Born in Bethlehem.

3. . . . I will send thee three by three.
   Well, three was the three men riding,
   Two was the Paul and Silas, . . .

4. . . . I will send thee four by four.
   Well, four was the four come a-knocking at the door,
   Three was the three men riding, . . .

5. . . . I will send thee five by five.
   Well, five was the Gospel preachers,
   Four was the four come a-knocking at the door, . . .

6. . . . I will send thee six by six.
   Well, six was the six that couldn't be fixed,
   Five was the Gospel preachers, . . .

7. . . . I will send thee seven by seven.
   Well, seven was the seven who went to heaven,
   Six was the six that couldn't be fixed, . . .

8. . . . I will send thee eight by eight.
   Well, eight was the eight who stood by the gate,
   Seven was the seven who went to heaven, . . .

9. . . . I will send thee nine by nine.
   Well, nine was the nine who saw the sign,
   Eight was the eight who stood by the gate, . . .

10. . . . I will send thee ten by ten.
    Well, ten was the Ten Commandments,
    Nine was the nine who saw the sign, . . .

A New Year's Carol

At New Year's time, children in Canada go from house to house to visit their neighbors. "Mistletoe Gifts" is one of the children's favorite songs.

Mistletoe Gifts

French-Canadian Carol

1. Luck to the mas - ter and the mis - tress,
2. Gifts for the New Year will be wel - come,

Luck to the peo - ple dwell - ing here,
Wel - come to us and luck to you,

Wheth - er a cot - tage or a cas - tle,
He who be - stows a New Year to - ken,

Luck to you all and good New Year!
Shall have good luck the whole year through.

REFRAIN

If we — please you with our sing - ing,

Sing - ing   loud   and   clear,

Out   of   the   cup-board gifts   be   bring-ing,

Gifts   to   give   us   cheer,

Luck   to   the   mas - ter   and   the   mis - tress,

Luck   to   you   all   and good New   Year!

Old Father Time

Old Father Time on New Year's Day
  Picked up his bag of months and years.
Thrust in his hand in a careless way,
  And pulled a wee fellow out by the ears.

"There you are," said he to the waiting crowd,
  "He's as good as any I have in my pack.
I never can tell, but I hope to be proud
  Of the little rascal when I come back."

Leroy F. Jackson

RIBBONS AND LACE

Can you make a valentine? The words of this song tell you how.

It's For My Valentine

Words and Music by Linda Williams

1. I think I'll start with a pa - per heart,
   leave some space for a bit of lace,
   if there's time, I'll in - vent a rhyme,

and I'll paint some flow - ers on it.
and I'll tie a rib - bon on it.
may - be e - ven write a son - net,

I'll make it all in my own de - sign,
And when it's done it'll __ look so fine!
Or some - thing sim - ple like "Please be mine."

1., 2.

It's for my val - en - tine.
It's for my val - en - tine.
It's for my val - en -

2. I'll
3. And

3.

slower

tine. Won't you be my val - en - tine?

Use this bell part to introduce the singing.

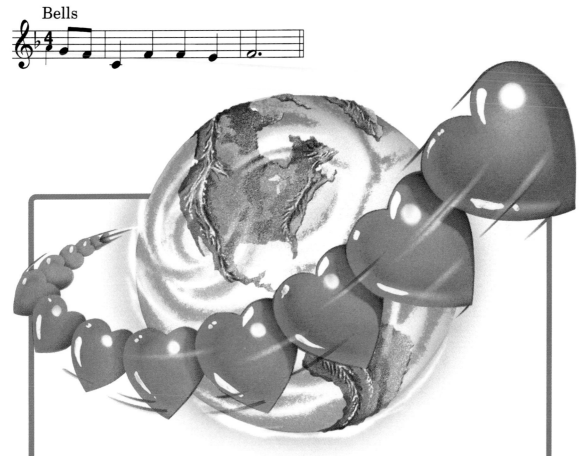

Bells

Valentine for Earth

Oh, it will be fine
To rocket through space
And see the reverse
Of the moon's dark face,

To travel to Saturn
Or Venus or Mars,
Or maybe discover
Some uncharted stars.

But do they have anything
Better than we?
Do you think, for instance,
They have a blue sea

For sailing and swimming?
Do planets have hills
With raspberry thickets
Where a song sparrow fills

The summer with music?
And do they have snow
To silver the roads
Where the school buses go?

Oh, I'm all for rockets
And worlds cold or hot,
But I'm wild in love
With the planet we've got!

Frances M. Frost

A Funny Valentine

How many times do you find this pattern in the song?

Never Gonna Be Your Valentine

Words and Music by Linda Williams

1. I don't wan-na be your val - en - tine,
2. I'm not gon-na be your val - en - tine,

   I don't wan-na be your val - en - tine,
   I'm not gon-na be your val - en - tine,

   Don't wan-na be your val - en - tine to - day!
   You're not the kind of val - en - tine I like!

   Oh, no, I don't wan-na be your val - en - tine,
   Oh, no, I'm not gon-na be your val - en - tine,

   I don't wan-na be your val - en - tine,
   I'm not gon-na be your val - en - tine,

Pack up your val - en - tine and go a - way!
Pack up your val - en - tine and take a hike!

You nev - er let me win at games,
You won't share this, you won't lend that.

You laugh at me and call me names,
Won't e - ven let me pet your cat!

So e - ven if you beg and plead and whine, _____
And yet you bor - row ev - 'ry - thing that's mine! _____

I'm nev - er gon - na be your val - en - tine! _____
I'm nev - er gon - na be your val - en - tine! _____

3. I might wanna be your valentine,
   I might wanna be your valentine,
   Don't tell a soul, 'cause you know very well
   If all my friends knew I was your valentine,
   They'd tease me and call me "Valentine,"
   That's why you have to promise not to tell!
   But you're so mean, you won't keep still!
   You'll tell them all, I know you will!
   So even though I think you're really fine,
   I'm never gonna be your valentine!

READING MUSIC

CARNELIAN

Marcus Uzilevsky

NAME THIS TUNE

Here is the solfa notation for a song you know. Can you guess what it is? To find out, clap and speak the rhythm syllables.

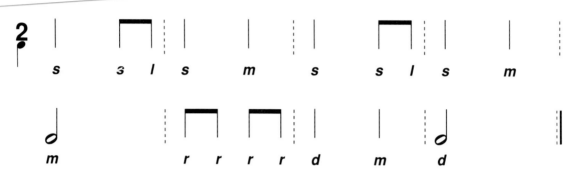

s   s   l   s   m   s   s   l   s   m

m   r   r   r   d   m   d

Add handsigns as you sing the solfa syllables.
Is the song written in phrases or motives?

SINGING WITH SOLFA SYLLABLES

Practice singing these pitches
then sing the song.

Knock the Cymbals

Texas Play-Party Game

Knock the cym - bals, do, oh, do,

Knock the cym - bals do, oh, do,

Knock the cym - bals do, oh, do,

Hel - lo Su - san Brown - o.

From SWING AND TURN: TEXAS PLAY-PARTY GAMES by William A. Owens. Copyright 1936 by Tardy Publishing Company. Reprinted by permission of McIntosh and Otis, Inc.

A FIVE-NOTE SCALE

How many pitches are used in this scale?

Sing it with solfa syllables and show handsigns.

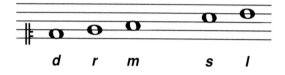

d   r   m   s   l

Another name for this five note scale is pentatonic.

This diagram shows a pentatonic scale.

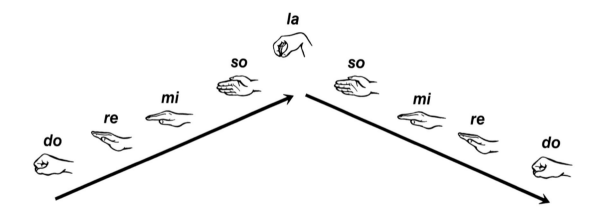

Can you read this melody?

From 333 Elementary Exercises (#240) by Zoltán Kodály. Copyright 1941 by Zoltán Kodály. Copyright renewed. English Edition © Copyright 1963 by Boosey & Co., Ltd. Reprinted by permission of Boosey & Hawkes, Inc.

WHERE IS *Do*?

Can you find the position of *do* on the staff? Try singing this tune with solfa syllables. Don't forget the repeat signs. Can you name this song?

MYSTERY SONG

Music by Lucille Wood

Two-Part Rhythm Piece

Here is a rhythm piece in two parts. Pat the beat as you think the rhythm of the bottom part.

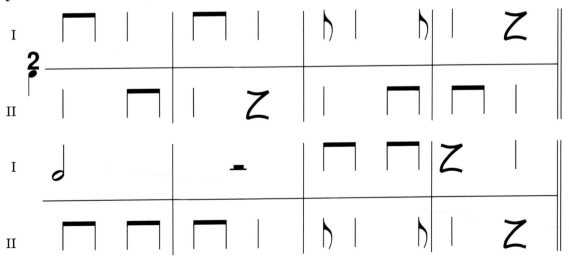

AN AMERICAN FOLK SONG

Read the words of "Old Aunt Dinah."
Which words repeat in each verse?

Old Aunt Dinah

Folk Song from North Carolina   Adapted by Jill Trinka

Old   Aunt   Di - nah   hoe   peas,   hoe   peas,

Old   Aunt   Di - nah   hoe   peas,   hoe.

2. Summer's getting hotter, hoe peas, hoe peas,
   Summer's getting hotter, hoe peas, hoe.

3. Winter's getting colder, hoe peas, hoe peas,
   Winter's getting colder, hoe peas, hoe.

4. So I'm gonna leave you, hoe peas, hoe peas,
   So I'm gonna leave you, hoe peas, hoe.

From COLLECTION OF NORTH CAROLINA FOLKLORE by Frank C. Brown.
Used by permission of Duke University Press.

VERSE AND REFRAIN

Here is a song for two groups of singers. One group can sing the refrain, the other can sing the verses.

Hill an' Gully

Calypso from Jamaica   English Words by Margaret Marks

Refrain: Hill an' gully rider,
           Hill an' gully.
           Hill an' gully rider,
           Hill an' gully.

1. Took my horse an' come down,
   Hill an' gully.
   But my horse done stumble down,
   Hill an' gully.
   An' the night-time come an' tumble down,
   Hill an' gully. *(Refrain)*

2. Oh the moon shine bright down,
   Hill an' gully.
   Ain't no place to hide in down,
   Hill an' gully.
   An' a zombie come a-ridin' down,
   Hill an' gully. *(Refrain)*

3. Oh, my knees they shake down,
   Hill an' gully.
   An' my heart starts quakin' down,
   Hill an' gully.
   Ain't nobody goin' to get me down,
   Hill an' gully. *(Refrain)*

4. That's the last I set down,
   Hill an' gully,
   Pray the Lord don' let me down,
   Hill an' gully.
   An' I run till daylight breakin' down,
   Hill an' gully. *(Refrain)*

FOUR-PART CANON

Sing this exercise in 4 parts.

4. **d¹** _____

3. **s** _____

2. **m** _____

1. **d** _____

Can you find the numbers that tell where each part starts to sing in this four-part canon?

Morning Bells

Traditional Round

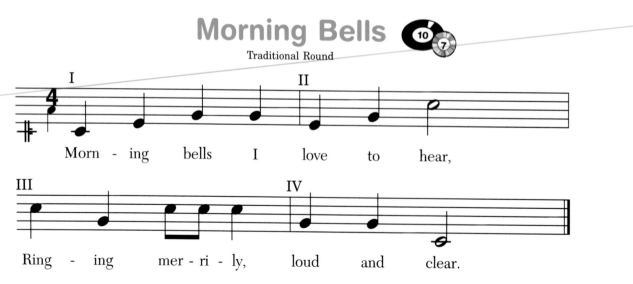

Morn - ing bells I love to hear,

Ring - ing mer - ri - ly, loud and clear.

KEEP THE BEAT

Feel the steady beat as you clap the rhythm of this song.

Tideo

Texas Play Party

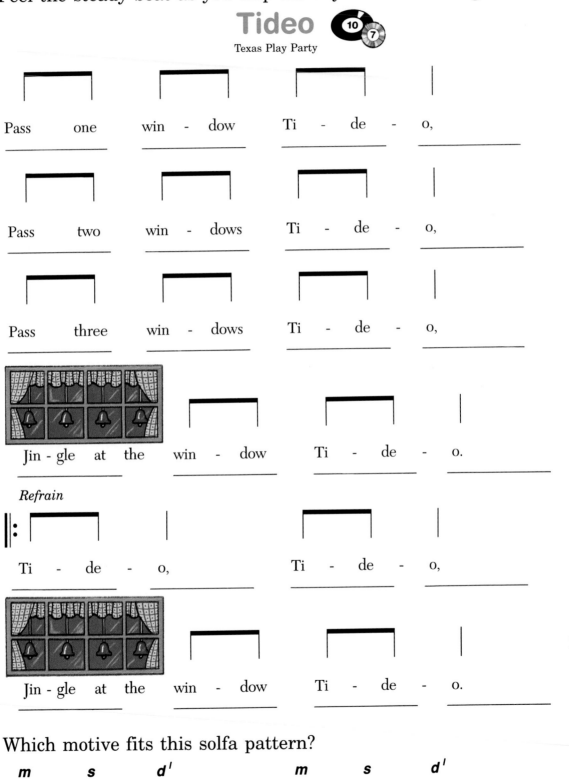

Pass   one   win - dow   Ti - de - o,

Pass   two   win - dows   Ti - de - o,

Pass   three   win - dows   Ti - de - o,

Jin - gle at the win - dow   Ti - de - o.

Refrain

Ti - de - o,   Ti - de - o,

Jin - gle at the win - dow   Ti - de - o.

Which motive fits this solfa pattern?

m   *s*   *d'*   *m*   *s*   *d'*

This famous mountain pass was the main road
used by pioneer settlers heading west.
Can you find the Cumberland Gap on a map?

Cumberland Gap

Kentucky Play Party   Collected and Adapted by Jill Trinka

1. Lay down, boys, take a little nap,
   Lay down, boys, take a little nap,
   Lay down, boys, take a little nap,
   Fortyone miles to Cumberland Gap,

Refrain: Cumberland Gap, Cumberland Gap,
   Ooo, Hoo, Way low down in Cumberland Gap

2. Cumberland Gap is a mighty fine place, *(3 times)*
   Three kinds of water to wash your face, *Refrain*

3. Cumberland Gap with its cliffs and rocks, *(3 times)*
   Home of the panther, bear, and fox, *Refrain*

4. Me and my wife and my wife's grandpap, *(3 times)*
   We raise Cain at Cumberland Gap, *Refrain*

A NEW RHYTHM

Clap the rhythm of "Paw Paw Patch" as you sing.

Paw Paw Patch

Singing Game from Kentucky

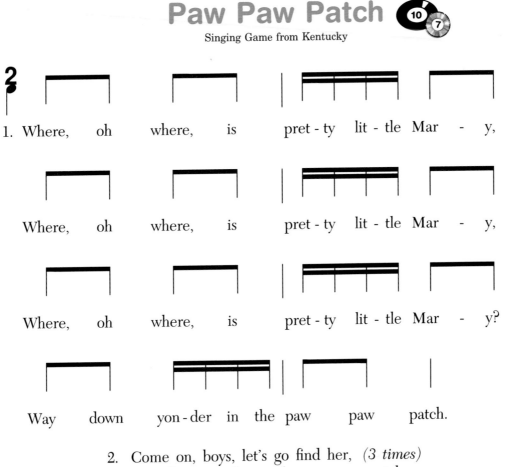

1. Where, oh where, is pret-ty lit-tle Mar - y,

Where, oh where, is pret-ty lit-tle Mar - y,

Where, oh where, is pret-ty lit-tle Mar - y?

Way down yon-der in the paw paw patch.

2. Come on, boys, let's go find her, *(3 times)*
   Way down yonder in the paw paw patch.

3. Pickin' up paw paws, put 'em in your pocket, *(3 times)*
   Way down yonder in the paw paw patch.

The rhythm in the color box is new.

 = 4 even sounds in one beat

Is the new rhythm in the second verse of "Paw Paw Patch?"

CONDUCTING THE METER

Conduct meter in 2 as you sing this song.

Dinah

Early American Folk Song

No one's in the house but Di - nah, Di - nah,

No one's in the house but me I know,

No one's in the house but Di - nah, Di - nah,

Strum-min' on the old ban - jo.

CROSSING THE RIVER

Sing this song to find out how the ducks crossed the river.

All the Ducks

Folk Song from the Netherlands
Adapted with New Words by Jill Trinka

1. "All the ducks are swimming in the water,"
   Fol-de-rol-de-rol-do, fol-de-rol-de-rol-do,
   "All the ducks are swimming in the water,"
   Fol-de-rol-de-rol-de-ray.

2. "The bridge is broken, how can we cross over?"
   Fol-de-rol-de-rol-do, fol-de-rol-de-rol-do,
   "The bridge is broken, how can we cross over?"
   Fol-de-rol-de-rol-de-ray.

3. "In my boat I'll ferry you right over," . . .

4. "Three new pennies, we will gladly pay you," . .

5. "I will take the money you have offered," . . .

6. In the boat they crossed the little river, . . .

Sing the rhythm syllables for "All the Ducks."

The name for ⌢ is fermata. It tells musicians to hold
the note a little longer.

TEXAS PLAY PARTY SONG

"Tideo" can be performed in three different ways.

Try all three.

- Sing the words.
- Sing the rhythm syllables.
- Sing the solfa syllables and show the handsigns.

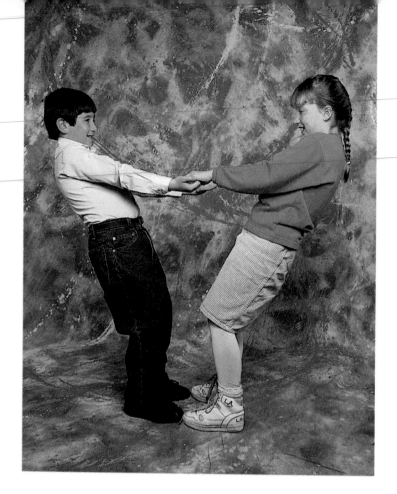

Tideo

Texas Play Party

do re mi so la do'

Pass one win-dow Ti - de - o, Pass two win-dows Ti - de - o,

Pass three win-dows Ti - de - o, Jin-gle at the win-dow Ti - de - o.

REFRAIN

Ti - de - o, Ti - de - o, Jin-gle at the win-dow Ti - de - o.

JUST LIKE THAT

What kind of "pumpkin" face will you make at the very end of this song?

do re mi so la

Pumpkin, Pumpkin

Traditional

Pump - kin, Pump - kin round and fat

Turn in - to a jack - o' - lan - tern just like that!

From THE SONG GARDEN by Carol Quimby Heath. Published by the Kodály Musical Training Institute. Used by permission.

Clap this ostinato as you sing.

A PIECE FOR TWO GROUPS

Look at the two parts below. How are they alike?
How are they different?

I
d d d d r r r m m m m s   m m m m r r r d d m m d

II
d   r   m   d   d   r   d

Clap the rhythm of this melody.

do   re   mi

Practice Piece

A NEW SOUND

There is a note missing in the notation of this melody.
Is the missing pitch higher or lower than *do*?

Billy In His Old Blue Jeans

Folk Song from North Carolina

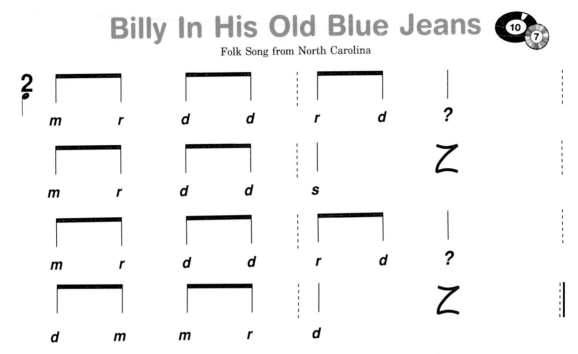

From FOLK SONGS OF THE SOUTHERN APPALACHIANS by Cecil Sharp. Used courtesy of Oxford University Press.

TRACE THE SHAPE

This song is shown in solfa notation. Use your finger to trace the shape of the melody. Can you show the handsign for the new sound?

Poor Little Kitty Cat

Folk Song from North Carolina

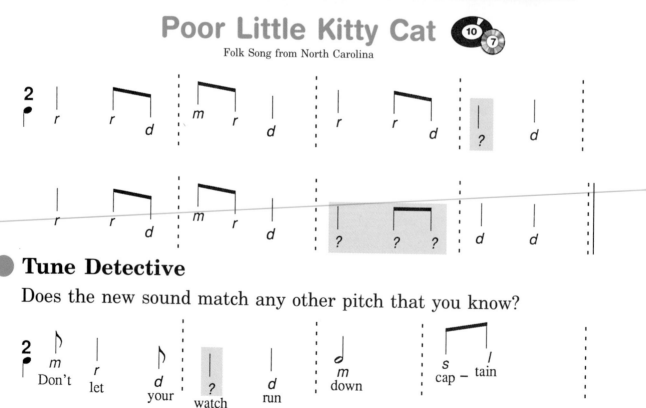

Tune Detective

Does the new sound match any other pitch that you know?

SINGING LOW *LA*

Here is the first phrase of "Billy in His Old Blue Jeans," shown with handsigns. Practice singing the phrase with handsigns and solfa syllables.

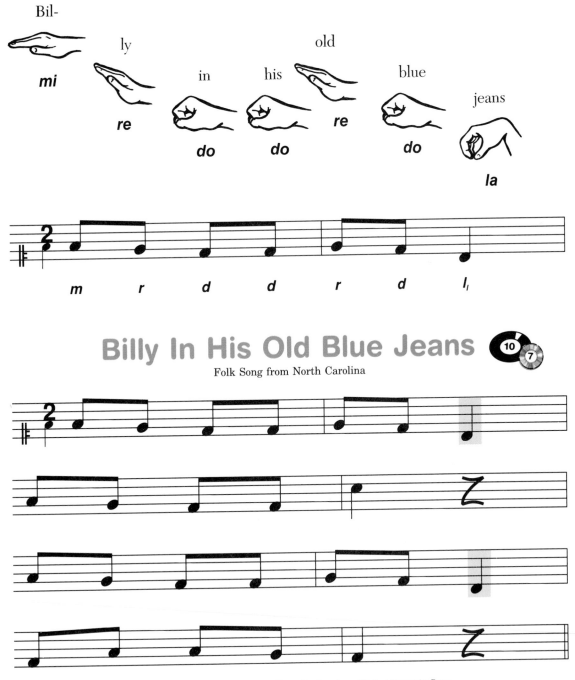

Billy In His Old Blue Jeans

Folk Song from North Carolina

From FOLK SONGS OF THE SOUTHERN APPALACHIANS by Cecil Sharp. Used courtesy of Oxford University Press.

TUNE DETECTIVE

l, d r m s l

Each of the phrases below
is from a song that you know.
Can you name the songs?

1.

Music by Margaret E. McGhee

2.

© 1983 Magna Music-Baron Inc., 10370 Page Industrial Boulevard, St. Louis MO 63132. Used by permission.

3.

4.

Collected and adapted by Jill Trinka. © 1989 Jill Trinka. All rights reserved.

What about this motive?

5.

Collected, adapted and arranged by John A. Lomax and Alan Lomax. TRO-© Copyright 1941 (renewed) Ludlow Music, Inc., New York, N.Y. Used by permission.

TAP THE BEAT—READ THE RHYTHM

Tap a steady beat as you read the rhythm of this song. Next, sing the song with the words. Now, sing with solfa syllables.

The Open Plain

Traditional   Arapahoe Indian   Words by William Littlebear

1. On the o - pen plain, buf - fa - lo, buf - fa - lo,

Hear the thund'ring herd, buf - fa - lo, buf - fa - lo,

Hi - yo! Hi - yo!

2. On the open plain,
   antelope, antelope,
   Grazing peacefully,
   antelope, antelope,
   Hi-yo! Hi-yo!

3. On the open plain,
   running deer, running deer,
   Leaping all about,
   running deer, running deer,
   Hi-yo! Hi-yo!

FAR FROM HOME

This song tells about being far from home.
Read the words to find out about the places
and things the songwriter misses most.

Land of the Silver Birch

Folk Song from Canada

1. Land of the silver birch, home of the beaver,
   Where still the mighty moose wanders at will.
   Blue lake and rocky shore, I will return once more,
   Boom de de boom boom, Boom de de boom boom,
   Boom de de boom boom, Boom.

2. Down in the forest, deep in the lowlands,
   My heart cries out for thee, hills of the north.
   Blue lake and rocky shore, I will return once more,
   Boom de de boom boom, Boom de de boom boom,
   Boom de de boom boom, Boom.

3. High on a rocky ledge, I'll build my wigwam,
   Close by the water's edge, silent and still,
   Blue lake and rocky shore, I will return once more,
   Boom de de boom boom, Boom de de boom boom,
   Boom de de boom boom, Boom.

From a collection by Edith Fowke. Used by permission.

A SONG FROM AFRICA

Here is a song for a leader and a group of singers. Look at the notation. What can you discover about the part the group sings?

Before Dinner

From the Belgian Congo

Solo

Chorus

First we go to hoe our gar - den, Ya, ya, ya, ya.
Next we car - ry jugs of wa - ter, Ya, ya, ya, ya.

Solo

Chorus

Then we pound the yel - low corn, Ya, ya, ya, ya.
Then we stir our pots of mush, Ya, ya, ya, ya.

Solo

Chorus

Now we eat come ga - ther 'round the camp-fire, Ya, ya, ya, ya.

LOWER THAN LOW *LA*

This song uses a new sound. It is lower than *la₁*.
Look through the notation. Can you find the new
solfa syllables?

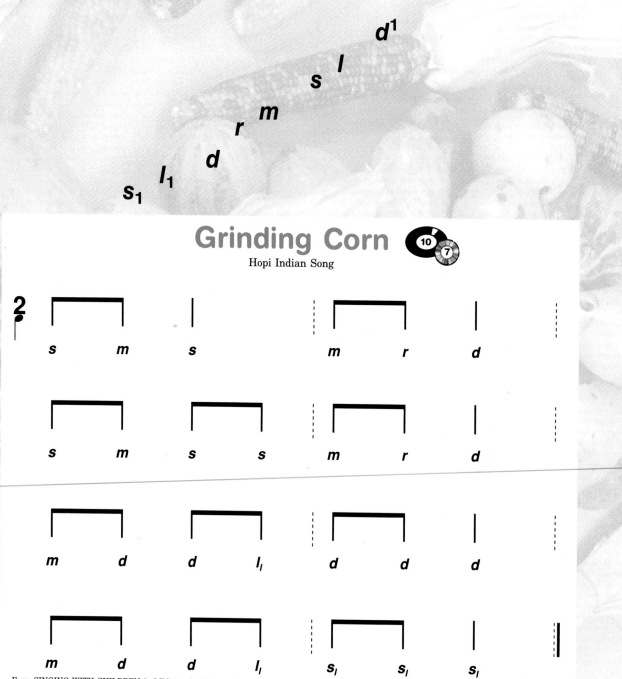

d¹

s *l*

r *m*

d

s₁ *l₁*

Grinding Corn

Hopi Indian Song

10 7

2

s   m   s   m   r   d

s   m   s   s   m   r   d

m   d   d   l₁   d   d   d

m   d   d   l₁   s₁   s₁   s₁

A New Note—Low *So*

Look at the color box and find the new note on the staff.

s͵ l͵ **d r m s**

Can you find low *so* in "Alabama Gal?"

COWBOY SINGING (detail)
Thomas Eakins

Alabama Gal

Folk Song from Alabama

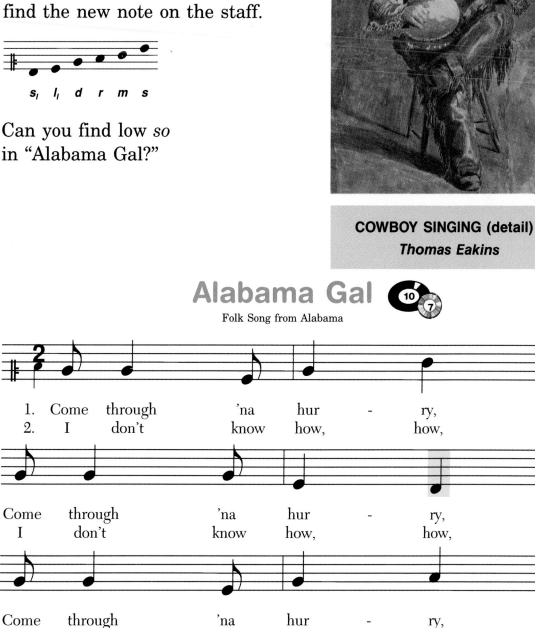

1. Come through 'na hur - ry,
2. I don't know how, how,

Come through 'na hur - ry,
I don't know how, how,

Come through 'na hur - ry,
I don't know how, how,

Al - a - bam - a Gal.
Al - a - bam - a Gal.

RHYTHM DETECTIVE

Sing this familiar song
with the words.

Melchior and Balthazar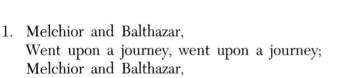

Folk Song from France   English Words by Emily Vidal

1. Melchior and Balthazar,
   Went upon a journey, went upon a journey;
   Melchior and Balthazar,
   Went upon a journey far with King Gaspar.

2. When they came to Bethlehem,
   They opened up the baskets, opened up the baskets;
   When they came to Bethlehem,
   They opened up the baskets they had brought with them.

3. Then they ate some cabbage soup.
   They were very hungry, oh, so very hungry;
   Then they ate some cabbage soup,
   They were just as hungry as they could be.

Which of the rhythm parts shown below matches the
rhythm of the words, part I or part II?

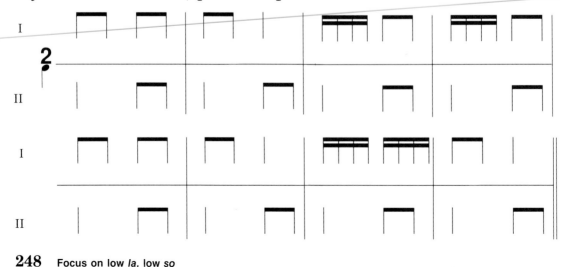

RING THE BELLS

Clap the rhythm of the melody as you sing this song.

Ring, Bells

Traditional German Carol

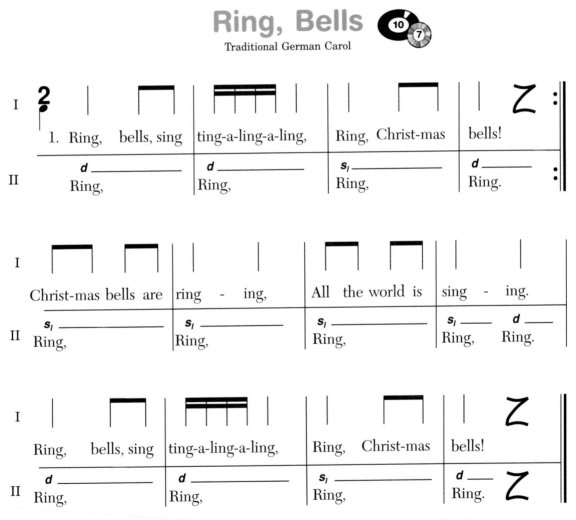

I
1. Ring, bells, sing ting-a-ling-a-ling, Ring, Christ-mas bells!

II
Ring, *d* ___ Ring, *d* ___ Ring, *s₁* ___ Ring. *d* ___

I
Christ-mas bells are ring - ing, All the world is sing - ing.

II
Ring, *s₁* ___ Ring, *s₁* ___ Ring, *s₁* ___ Ring, *s₁* ___ Ring. *d* ___

I
Ring, bells, sing ting-a-ling-a-ling, Ring, Christ-mas bells!

II
Ring, *d* ___ Ring, *d* ___ Ring, *s₁* ___ Ring. *d* ___

2. Ring, bells sing ting-a-ling-a-ling, Ring, Christmas bells! *(2 times)*
   May our hearts be merry, Joyful tidings carry,
   Ring, bells, sing ting-a-ling-a-ling, Ring Christmas bells!

Focus on low *la*, low *so*   249

PARTY IN THE BARN

Clap and sing the rhythm syllables of verse 1. When you sing verse 1 again, clap the rhythm and sing inside.

Goin' to the Party
Traditional Illinois Play Party

1. Goin' to the party in the old farm wagon,
   Goin' to the party in the old farm wagon,
   Goin' to the party in the old farm wagon,
   Get up, dapple grey.

2. One spring's broke and another one's saggin', . . .
   Get up, dapple grey.

3. One wheel's off, and another one's saggin', . . .
   Get up, dapple grey.

4. Fill up the bed with straw at the bottom, . . .
   Get up, dapple grey.

5. Come on, my beauties, let's go a-trottin', . . .
   Get up, dapple grey.

6. All the way home without upsettin', . . .
   Get up, dapple grey.

7. Good-bye girls, I'm glad I met you, . . .
   Get up, dapple grey.

LOW *LA* AND LOW *SO*

In this song, *do* is in the first space.
Can you find low *la* and low *so*?

s_l l_l d r m s l

Chicken on the Fence Post

Play Party Song

1. Chick-en on the fence post, can't dance Jo - sey,

Chick-en on the fence post, can't dance Jo - sey,

Chick-en on the fence post, can't dance Jo - sey,

Hel - lo Su - san Brown - y - o.

2. Choose your partner and come dance Josey, . . .

3. Chew my gum while I dance Josey, . . .

4. Shoestring's broke and I can't dance Josey, . . .

5. Hold my mule while I dance Josey, . . .

6. Hair in the butter, can't dance Josey, . . .

7. Briar in my heels, can't dance Josey, . . .

8. Stumped my toe, can't dance Josey, . . .

From A BOOK OF NONSENSE SONGS by Norman Cazdon. Published by Abelard-Schuman, 1958.

SING AND CLAP

Sing the melody of "Hold My Mule" with solfa syllables. Then clap the rhythm as you sing all three verses with the words.

Hold My Mule

10 7

African-American Folk Song

1. Hold my mule while I dance Jo - sey.

Hold my mule while I dance Jo - sey.

Hold my mule while I dance Jo - sey.

Oh, Miss Su - san Brown.

2. Wouldn't give a nickel if I
   couldn't dance Josey. (*3 times*)
   Oh, Miss Susan Brown.

3. Had a glass of buttermilk and
   I danced Josey. (*repeat 3 times*)
   Oh, Miss Susan Brown.

From ON THE TRAIL OF NEGRO FOLKSONGS by Dorothy
Scarborough Harvard University Press. Copyright, 1925
by Harvard University Press. Copyright, 1953 by
Mary McDaniel Parker. Reprinted by permission.

TAPPING RHYTHMS

Tap this rhythm with your left hand.

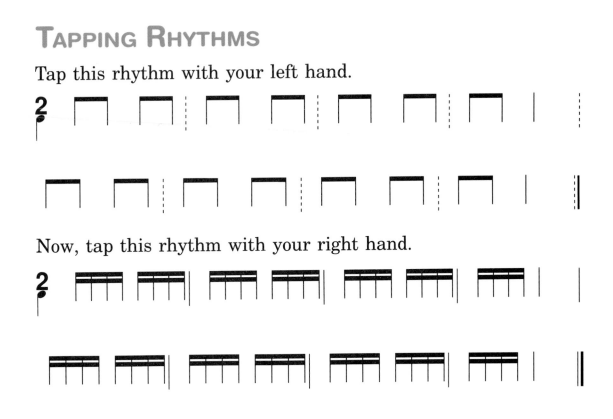

Now, tap this rhythm with your right hand.

● Combining Rhythms

Listen to how a Russian composer Dmitri Kabalevsky
used these two rhythms in a piece for the piano.
Conduct meter in 2 as you listen.

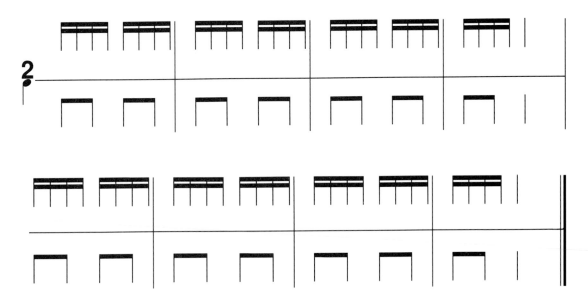

WORKIN' ON THE LEVEE

When a river overflowed, workers built
levees to hold back the water. The workers
depend on their boss (captain) to watch
carefully so they don't work overtime.

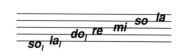

Don't Let Your Watch Run Down

South Texas Work Song

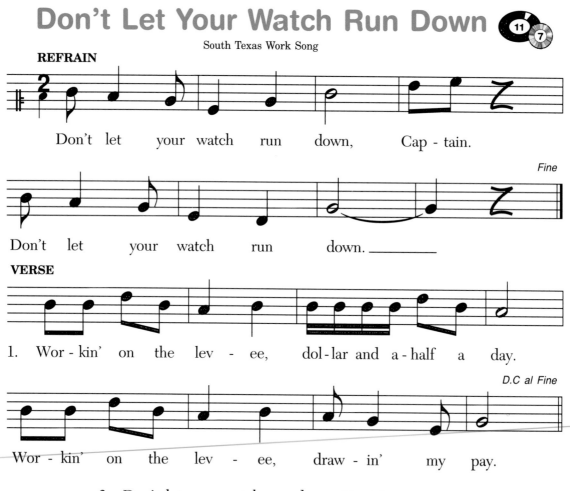

2. Don't let your watch run down, Captain,
   Don't let your watch run down,
   Workin' on the railroad, mud up to my knees,
   Workin' on the railroad, tryin' to please.

3. Refrain
   When you see me comin', hoist your window high,
   When you see me leavin', bow down and cry.

LET'S PLAY RECORDER

Use the fingering chart below
and practice playing
mi, *re*, and *do* on your recorder.

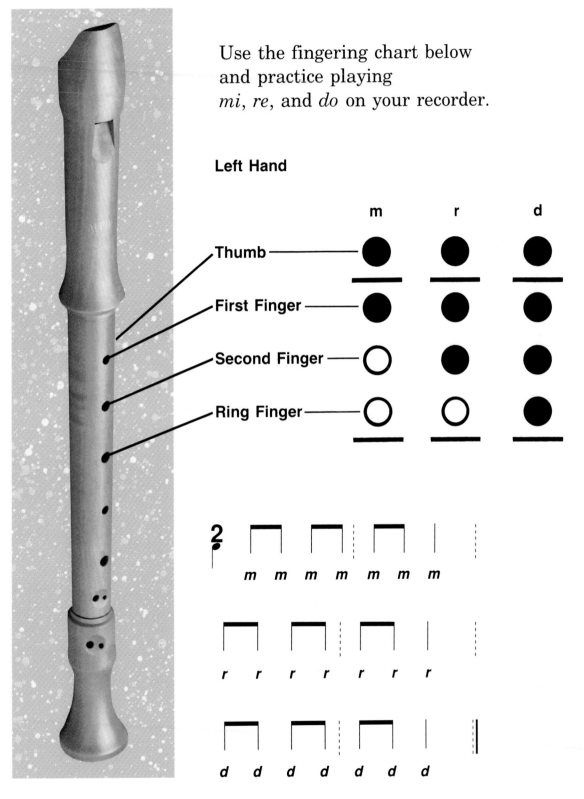

Left Hand

SING AND PLAY

Sing and play
these examples
with solfa syllables.

Sing this two-line piece in
solfa. Show handsigns.

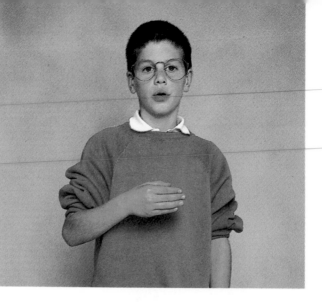

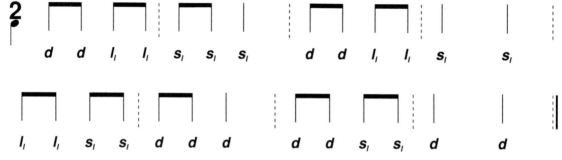

d d l, l, s, s, s,   d d l, l, s,   s,

l, l, s, s, d d d   d d s, s, d   d

● Sing from Staff Notation

d   l,   s,

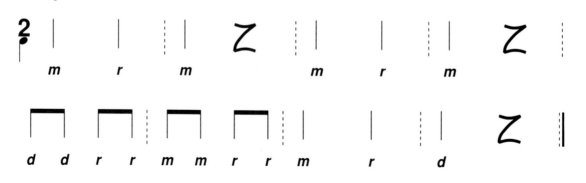

● Play on Recorder

m   r   m   m   r   m

d d r r m m r r m   r   d

"Great Big House" is arranged
for two groups of singers.
Sing each part separately,
then with your classmates,
put both parts together.

Great Big House

Louisiana Play Party Song

1. Great big house in New Or - leans, For - ty sto - ries high;

1.	Great,	great big house, Great,	great big house;
2.	Old,	old mill-stream, Old,	old mill-stream;
3.	Fare,	fare-thee-well, Fare,	fare-thee-well;

Ev - 'ry room that I been in, Filled with pump-kin pie.

Great,	great big house	in	New Or - leans.
Old,	old mill-stream	old	mill - stream.
Fare,	fare - thee - well	Fare	fare - thee - well.

2. Went down to the old millstream
   To fetch a pail of water,
   Put one arm around my wife,
   The other 'round my daughter.

3. Fare-thee-well, my darling girl,
   Fare-thee-well, my daughter,
   Fare-thee-well, my darling girl
   With the golden slippers on her.

NEW NOTES FOR RECORDER

Look at the diagram below and find some new notes to play on your recorder.

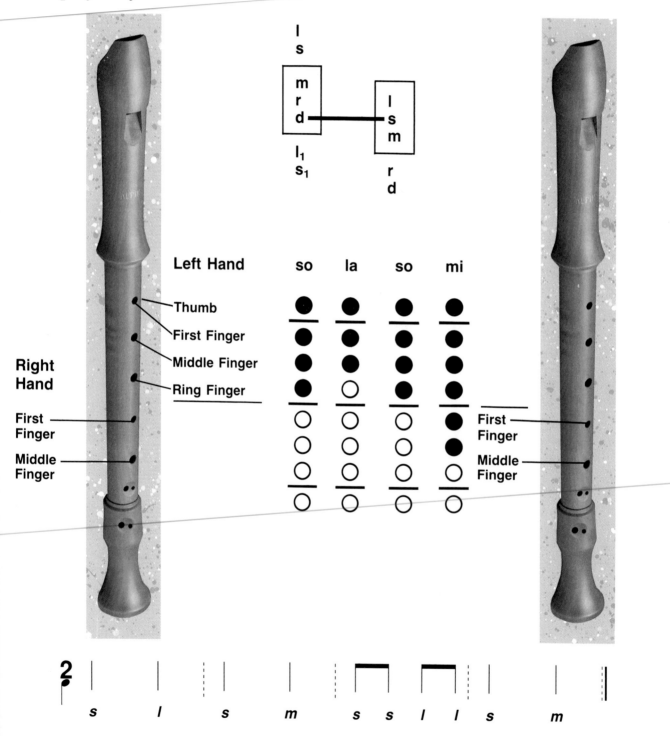

READ THE RHYTHM—READ THE TUNE

Tap the beat and say the rhythm syllables. Then sing the tune inside and show the handsigns. Sing the last note aloud.

Never Sleep Late Anymore

American Folk Song

From Music for Young Americans I. Used courtesy of D.C. Heath and Co.

● Phrase Detective

Look at the staff below. It shows the notation for one of the phrases you just sang. Can you tell which phrase it is?

LOOK OUT!

Find a partner and try singing "Scotland's Burning" as a two-part round.

Scotland's Burning

Traditional Round

I
Scot - land's burn - ing, Scot - land's burn - ing,

II
Look out! Look out!

III
Fire! Fire! Fire! Fire!

IV
Pour on wa - ter, Pour on wa - ter!

WHO DO YOU LOVE?

Love Somebody

American Folk Song

1. Love somebody, yes, I do!
   Love somebody, yes, I do.
   Love somebody, yes, I do.
   Love somebody, but I won't tell who!

2. Twice sixteen is thirty two, (3 times)
   Sally won't you love me, do, girl, do!

3. Sun comes up and the moon goes down. (3 times)
   See my little girl in her evening gown.

4. Somebody come and find me gone. (3 times)
   They better leave my girl alone.

5. Love somebody, sure and true, (3 times)
   Love somebody and it may be you!

© 1965 Jean Ritchie, Gordie Music Publishing Company. Used by permission.

● Tune Detective

Which example shows the melody for the phrase
"love somebody but I won't tell who"?

SING AND SIGN

Practice singing and signing each part of the example below. Find a partner and sing the parts together.

```
I    d    m    s    m    d    m    r
II   d ____    s₁ ____    d ____    s₁

I    d    m    s    m    r    m    d
II   d ____    s₁ ____    s₁ ____    d
```

You can use d and s_1 to make a second part for the song "Dinah."

Dinah

Early American Folk Song

No one's in the house but Di-nah, Di-nah, No one's in the house but me, I know,

No one's in the house but Di-nah, Di-nah, Strum-min' on the old ban - jo.

"SILENT" SINGING

Sing this song "silently" by singing inside and showing handsigns. Now, sing the song aloud with the nonsense words.

s₁ d r m s l

Fadding Gidding

West African Lullaby   Adapted by Jill Trinka

Fad-ding gid-ding, fad-ding go,   San - te' mo - le' San - te' mo - le',

Fad-ding gid-ding, fad-ding go,   Ev-er since I born my hand done so.

From SING IT YOURSELF by Louis Bradford. © 1978 Alfred Publishing Company. Used by permission of the publisher.

● **Tune Detective**

What song do you know that starts like this?

4

d r m d d r m d

And ends like this?

d s₁ d   d s₁ d

THE MUSIC ALPHABET

The music alphabet has seven letters.

A B C D E F G

Each note on the staff has its own absolute letter name. These names are determined by the G clef sign on the staff.

Look at the staff below and notice that the clef makes a circle around the second line. This line is called *G*.

If we know where the note *G* is located, then we can figure out the names of all of the other notes on the staff.

B C D E F G A B C D E F G A

Notes going up on the staff go forward in the alphabet.

Notes going down on the staff go backward in the alphabet.

Play the Recorder

You can play $B \cdot A \cdot G$ on the recorder. Look at the diagram below and practice the fingerings.

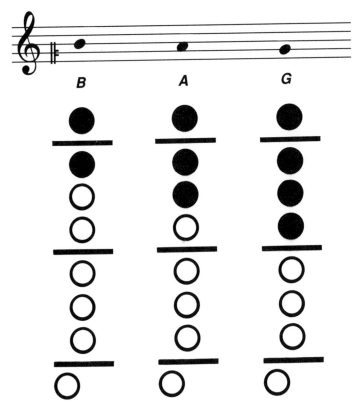

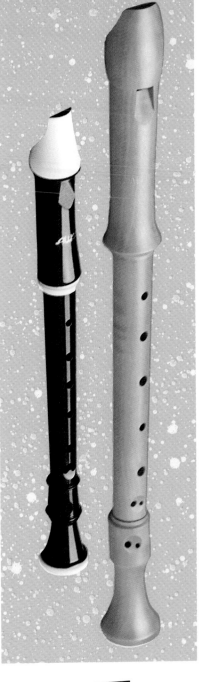

Sing the solfa syllables, then the letter names as you finger the notes on your recorder. Use the fingering position.

Sing the same song, but use C as *do*. Sing with solfa syllables, then letter names.

Do in Three Places

Use the fingering position on your recorder to sightread "Hosisipa." You will be reading m, r, d and l_1 in three different places on the staff. Sing the solfa syllables as you practice the fingerings.

From SING IT YOURSELF by Louis Bradford © 1978. Alfred Publishing Company. Used by permission of the publisher.

● Note Detective

There is one note that is used in each of the three examples. Can you find it? What is the letter name of the note?

What solfa syllable name does the note A have when:

1. $G = do$?
2. $C = do$?
3. $F = do$?

SING AND DANCE

Conduct meter in 2 and say rhythm syllables.
Sing with handsigns and solfa syllables.

Seminole Duck Dance

Seminole Indian Dance

(drum)

SINGING IN CANON

Sing this song with solfa syllables.
Then find a partner and sing in canon.

Canoe Song

Words and Music by Margaret E. McGhee

1. My pad - dle's keen and bright, Flash-ing with sil - ver.

Fol - low the wild goose flight, Dip, dip and swing.

2. Dip, dip and swing her back, Flashing with silver.
Swift as the wild goose flies, Dip, dip and swing.

FUR TRADERS DESCENDING THE MISSOURI (detail)   *George Caleb Bingham*

PARTNER SONGS

Partner songs are two songs that can be sung together. "Canoe Song" and "Land of the Silver Birch" can be sung as partner songs.

Land of the Silver Birch

Folk Song from Canada

1. Land of the sil-ver birch, home of the bea - ver,

Where still the might-y moose wan-ders at will,

Blue lake and rock-y shore, I will re - turn once more.

Boom de de boom boom, Boom de de boom boom, Boom de de boom boom

Boom.

From a collection by Edith Fowke. Used by permission.

TALL AND MIGHTY TREES

Have fun singing this song 3 different ways:
- Sing with solfa syllables.
- Sing with absolute letter names.
- Sing all the verses with the words.

In the Forest

African Christmas Carol   English Words by Jill Trinka

In the for - est dark   and   qui - et,

In the for - est dark   and   qui - et,

Here   I   sit   in   won - der,

Here   I   sit   in   peace.

2. Oh, the trees are tall and mighty,
   Oh, the trees are tall and mighty,
   Reaching up and outward,
   Reaching to the sky.

3. In the distance birds are calling,
   In the distance birds are calling,
   Come fly away with me,
   Come fly away with me.

Piece for Two Players

Recorder Duet

Music by Zoltán Kodály   Arranged by Jill Trinka

A MOUNTAIN BALLAD

Try conducting meter in 4 as you sing the words of this famous ballad.

The Death of the Robin

Appalachian Ballad

1. Who killed the ___ Ro - bin?

Who killed the ___ Ro - bin?

"I," said the spar-row, "with my lit - tle bow and ar - row, It was

I, oh, ___ it was I."

2. Who saw him die? *(repeat)*
   "I," said the fly, "With my little teeny eye,
   It was I, oh, it was I."

3. Who dug his grave? *(repeat)*
   "I," said the crow, "With my little spade and hoe,
   It was I, oh, it was I."

4. Who sang his funeral? *(repeat)*
   "I," said the lark, "With a song and with a harp,
   It was I, oh, it was I."

Rockwell Kent, *Revisitation*, 1928, copyright 1990, Indianapolis Museum of Art, Daniel P. Erwin Fund

REVISITATION   *Rockwell Kent*

A RAIN SONG

Sing this song first with the words, then with solfa syllables.

l,   d   r   s   l
E   G   A   D   E

Breezes Are Blowing

Luiseno Indian Rain Chant

Breez-es are blow - ing, Blow-ing clouds of wa - ter;

On my face, rain - ing, Rain-ing from the o - cean;

Breez-es are blow - ing, Blow-ing clouds of wa - ter.

Clap this ostinato as you sing.
Then play it on a drum.

GREETINGS!

How do you greet your family and friends when you arrive home from school?

Home From School

Folk Song from China   English Words by David Eddleman

When the ___ sun is ___ sink - ing low,

Home - ward ___ from my school I ___ go,

There where ___ I know ___ I will find,

Wait - ing, ___ fa - ther and moth - er kind.

A NEW SCALE

You have sung songs whose ending tone is *do* or *la₁*. Can you name the final pitch in "Grinding Corn?"

Grinding Corn

Hopi Indian Song

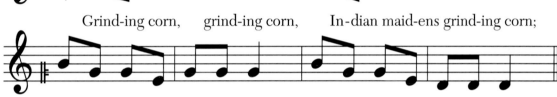

Grind-ing corn,   grind-ing corn,   In-dian maid-ens grind-ing corn;

God of rain and sun and sky,   Send the gen - tle but - ter - fly.

From SINGING WITH CHILDREN, 2nd Edition, by Robert and Vernice Nye, Neva Aubin, and George Kyme. © 1970, 1962 by Wadsworth Publishing Company, Inc. Used by permission of the publisher.

Sing the *so*-pentatonic scale: s_1, l_1, d, r, m, s

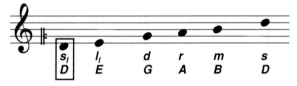

Here is another melody that ends on s_1.
Does it have all 5 notes of the so_1 pentatonic scale?

Yoop Biddy

Southern Plantation Song

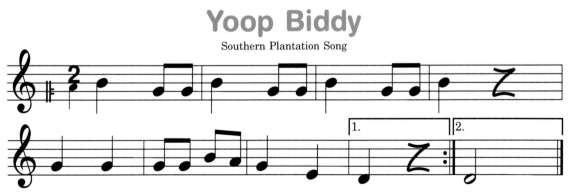

From SING IT YOURSELF by Louis Bradford. © 1978 Alfred Publishing Company. Used by permission of the publisher.

CREATE AN OSTINATO

Tap a steady beat as you sing "Raccoon Dance Song." Create an ostinato for this song.

Raccoon Dance Song

Traditional Algonquin Indian

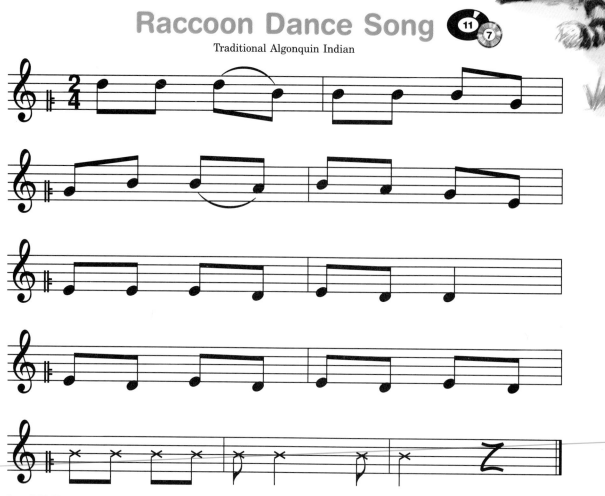

From SING IT YOURSELF by Louis Bradford. © 1978. Alfred Publishing Company. Used by permission.

● Can You Read This?

Match the solfa motives below with the motives in "Raccoon Dance Song."

1. *d - m - m - r - m - r - d - l₁*

2. *l₁ - s₁ - l₁ - s₁ - l₁ - s₁ - l₁ - s₁*

3. *l₁ - l₁ - l₁ - s₁ - l₁ - s₁ - s₁*

4. *s - s - s - m - m - m - m - d*

AN APPALACHIAN SONG

Notice that "Cotton-Eye Joe"
is written in *F = do*. Here
are the notes used in the song.

Cotton-Eye Joe

Folk Song from Tennessee

1. Where did you come from? Where did you go?

Where did you come from, Cot-ton-Eye — Joe?

2. I've come for to see you,
   I've come for to sing.
   I've come for to bring you
   A song and a ring.

3. When did you leave here?
   Where did you go?
   When you coming back here,
   Cotton-eye Joe?

4. Left here last winter,
   I've wandered through the year.
   Seen people dyin'
   Seen them with their fear.

5. I've been to the cities,
   Buildings cracking down.
   Seen the people calling,
   Falling to the ground.

6. I'll come back tomorrow,
   If I can find a ride.
   Or I'll sail in the breezes,
   Blowin' on the tide.

7. Well, when you do come back here
   Look what I have brung.
   A meadow to be run in,
   A song to be sung.

8. Where did you come from?
   Where did you go?
   Where did you come from,
   Cotton-eye Joe.

FUN IN THE SUN

Sing this song in both English and Spanish to discover what activity this family enjoys at the sea.

Let's Go to the Sea
(Vamos a la mar)

Folk Song from Guatemala

Let's go to the sea, ___ tum tum,
Va - mos a la mar, ___ tum tum,

Hook some fish and fry 'em, tum tum,
a co - mer pes - ca - do, tum tum,

Mouth as red as ru - by, tum tum,
Bo - ca co - lo - ra - da, tum tum,

Bar - be - cue or fry 'em, tum tum.
Fri - ti - to y a - sa - do, tum tum.
free - tee - toh ee ah - sah - doh toom toom

2. Let's go to the sea, tum tum,
   Catch a fish and grill it, tum tum,
   Barbecue or fry it, tum tum,
   In a wooden skillet, tum tum.

   Vamos a la mar, tum tum,
   A comer pescado, tum tum,
   Fritito y asado, tum tum,
   En sartèn de palo, tum tum.

Used by permission of the Organization of American States

A Two Part Song

Enjoy singing this song in two parts with your classmates.

In the Forest

African Christmas Carol   English Words by Jill Trinka

"Come, fly a-way with me. _____ Come fly a-way with me." __

"Fly a-way, Come fly a-way with me." __

SAND BANK WITH WILLOWS, MAGNOLIA (detail)   *William Morris Hunt*

TWO SONGS FROM CHINA

In this song, a young crow feeds his mother since she fed him when he was very small.

Song of the Crow

Folk Song from China

"Caw! caw! caw!" says the crow to me.

He loves the old ones I can see.

Birds grow __ old so they can't fly;

Son flut - ters out some __ worms to spy.

Mo - ther __ dear he feeds with care.

He nev - er minds he has no share.

My   moth - er   dear   she   once   fed   me.

"Caw!"   says   the   crow   up —   in   the   tree.

Scale Detective

Songs that use *do, re, mi, so* and *la* can end on different notes. The final note tells us which pentatonic scale the song uses. Which scale does the song "Frogs" use?

Frogs

Folk Song from China

Each   frog   has   a   sin - gle   mouth,
he   has   two   eyes   and   four   legs.

Pin,   pon,   pin,   pon,   Count   them —   with   me.

Dur - ing   times   of   peace,   frogs   do   not   drink.

Wa - ter   li - lies   float   on   the   pond.

ANIMALS, ANIMALS

Enjoy singing this song that contains both
low *la* and low *so*.

Who Built the Ark?

African-American Spiritual

Refrain: Who built the ark? Noah! Noah!
Who built the ark? Brother Noah built the ark!

Verses:
1. Now, didn't old Noah build the ark?
He built it out of a hickory bark.

2. He built it long, both wide and tall,
Plenty of room for the large and small,

3. Now in come the animals two by two,
Hippopotamus and kangaroo.

4. Now in come the animals three by three,
Two big cats and a bumble bee. *Refrain*

5. Now in come the animals four by four,
Two through the window and two through the door,

6. Now in come the animals five by five,
Four little sparrows and the redbird's wife.

7. Now in come the animals six by six,
Elephant laughed at the monkey's tricks,

8. Now in come the animals seven by seven,
Four from home and the rest from heaven. *Refrain*

9. Now in come the animals eight by eight,
Some were on time and the others were late.

NOAH'S ARK   *Edward Hicks*

10. Now in come the animals nine by nine,
    Some was a-shouting and some was a-crying.

11. Now in come the animals ten by ten,
    Five black roosters and five black hens,

12. Now Noah says, "Go shut that door,
    The rain's started dropping and we can't take more!" *Refrain*

PLAYING THE AUTOHARP

The picture shows you
the correct position for
playing the autoharp.

● Two-Chord Accompaniment

Follow these directions to play a two-chord
accompaniment.
- Place your left index finger on the button marked *F*.
- Place your left middle finger on the button marked C_7.
- Look at the chord pattern below. It shows when to
  press each button.
- As you press the buttons, use your right hand to
  strum the strings. Make each strum last for two beats.

F C_7 F C_7 F

You can use the F and C_7 chord pattern to
accompany the song "Sandy Land," page 108.

Three-Chord Accompaniment

Follow these directions to play a three-chord accompaniment.

- Place your left index finger on the button marked C.
- Place your left middle finger on the button marked G_7.
- Place your left ring finger on the button marked F.
- Look at the chord pattern below. It shows when to press each button.
- As you press the buttons, use your right hand to strum the strings. Make each strum last for two beats.

You can use the C, G_7, and F chord pattern to accompany the song "Shuckin' of the Corn," page 6.

Follow the Chord Names

Try playing an accompaniment for other two- and three-chord songs. The chord names in the music will tell you which buttons to press and when to change from one chord to another.

- Old Joe Clark, page 36
- Billy Boy, page 88
- Bow, Belinda, page 109
- Polly Wolly Doodle, page 124
- My Home's in Montana, page 20
- All Night, All Day, page 50

PLAYING THE RECORDER

Using your left hand, cover the holes shown in the first diagram.

Cover the tip of the mouthpiece with your lips. Blow gently as you whisper "daah." You will be playing *B*.

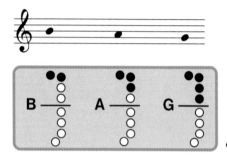

When you can play B, A, and G, you will be able to play melody 1.

Practice playing two new notes— high C and high D. When you can play them, you are ready to try melody 2 at the top of the next page.

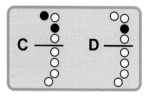

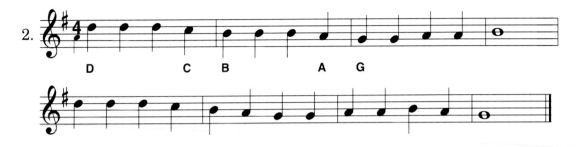

2.

Here are four new notes to practice. When you can play them, you will be ready to try melody 3.

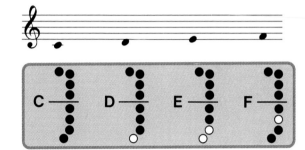

3.

Using the notes you have learned so far, you will be able to play some songs in your book. Try one of these.
- H'Atira, page 12
- Alekoki, page 64
- Scotland's Burning, page 111
- The Jasmine Flower, page 158

Here are two new notes to practice—F♯ and B♭. When you can play them, you will be ready to try one of the songs listed below.

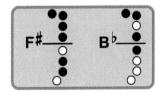

- The Little Bells of Westminster, page 62
- Little Boy of the Sheep, page 145
- Lovely Evening, page 63
- Brother John, page 107

THE SOUND BANK

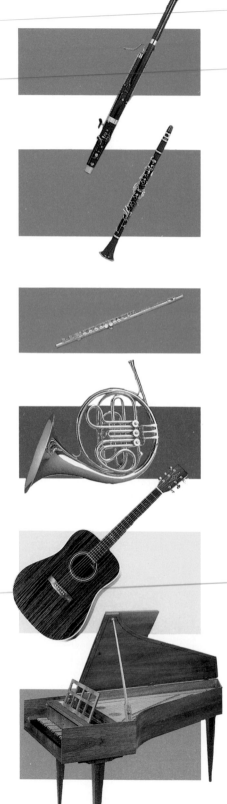

Bassoon A large tube-shaped wooden instrument with a double reed. Low notes on a bassoon can sound gruff and comical. Higher notes sound softer and sweeter. (p. 149)

Clarinet An instrument shaped like a long cylinder. It is usually made of wood and has a reed in the mouthpiece. The clarinet's low notes are soft and hollow. The highest notes are thin and piercing. (p. 127)

Flute A small metal instrument shaped like a pipe. The player holds the flute sideways and blows across an open mouthpiece. The flute's voice is clear and sweet. (p. 127)

French Horn A medium-sized instrument made of coiled brass tubing. At one end is a large "bell," at the other end a mouthpiece. The sound of the horn is mellow and warm. (p. 106)

Guitar A string instrument plucked with the fingers or a pick. A guitar can play a melody. It can also make chords to accompany a melody. Electric guitars sound much louder than regular guitars. They can also make many special sounds. (p. 121)

Harpsichord A keyboard instrument shaped something like a piano. When the keys are pressed, the strings inside the instrument are plucked by small quills. This gives the sound a tinkling quality. (p. 164)

Oboe A slender wooden instrument with a double reed. In its low voice, the oboe can sound mysterious. When it goes higher, the sound is thin and sweet.

Piano A large keyboard instrument with strings inside. When the keys are pressed, hammers inside the piano hit the strings. The piano can play very high and very low sounds, very soft and very loud sounds. (p. 100)

Recorder A simple wooden instrument. It has a "whistle" mouthpiece at one end and holes in the side that can be covered and uncovered to change pitches. The recorder comes in various sizes, the larger ones sounding lower, the smaller ones higher. (p. 126)

Trombone A fairly large brass instrument with a large "bell" at the end of the tubing and a long curved "slide." The trombone can be loud and brilliant, but its soft voice is mellow. (p. 127)

Trumpet A small brass instrument with a "bell" at the end of its coiled tubing. The trumpet's voice can be loud and bright, but can also sound warm and sweet. (p. 127)

Tuba A very large brass instrument with a wide "bell" at the end of coiled tubing. The tuba's low notes are soft and dark-sounding. The higher ones are full and warm. (p. 106)

GLOSSARY

AB form (p. 116) A musical plan that has two different parts, or sections.

ABA form (p. 118) A musical plan that has three sections. The first and last sections are the same. The middle section is different.

accompaniment (p. 33) Music that supports the sound of the featured performers.

ballad (p. 156) In music, a song that tells a story.

chord (p. 106) A group of three or more different tones played or sung together.

composer (p. 24) A person who makes up pieces by putting sounds together in his or her own way.

contrast (p. 121) Two or more things that are different. In music, slow is a contrast to fast; section A is a contrast to section B.

countermelody (p. 112) A melody that is played or sung at the same time as another melody.

dynamics (p. 145) The loudness and softness of sound.

form (p. 116) The overall plan of a piece of music.

harmony (p. 106) Two or more different tones sounding at the same time.

introduction (p. 13) In a song, music played before the singing begins.

leap (p. 98) To move from one tone to another, skipping over the tones in between.

lullaby (p. 66) A quiet song, often sung when rocking a child to sleep.

melody (p. 106) A line of single tones that move upward, downward, or repeat.

melody pattern (p. 35) An arrangement of pitches into a small grouping, usually occurring often in a piece.

meter (p. 82) The way the beats of music are grouped, often in sets of two or in sets of three.

mood (p. 100) The feeling that a piece of music gives. The *mood* of a lullaby is quiet and gentle.

notes (p. 91) Symbols for sound in music.

ostinato (p. 107) A rhythm or melody pattern that repeats.

partner songs (p. 108) Two or more different songs that can be sung at the same time to create harmony.

phrase (p. 51) A musical "sentence." Each *phrase* expresses one thought.

refrain (p. 32) The part of a song that repeats, using the same melody and words.

repeated tones (p. 92) Two or more tones in a row that have the same sound.

repetition (p. 121) Music that is the same, or almost the same, as music that was heard earlier.

rests (p. 91) Symbols for silences in music.

rhythm pattern (p. 117) A group of long and short sounds.

round (p. 110) A follow-the-leader process in which all sing the same melody but start at different times.

shantey (p. 26) A sailor's work song.

steady beat (p. 7) A regular pulse.

strong beat (p. 87) The first beat in a measure.

tempo (p. 76) The speed of the beat in music.

theme (p. 25) An important melody that occurs several times in a piece of music.

tone color (p. 124) The special sound that makes one instrument or voice sound different from another.

CLASSIFIED INDEX

FOLK AND TRADITIONAL SONGS

HOLIDAY AND SPECIAL OCCASION SONGS

SONG INDEX

ACKNOWLEDGMENTS

Credit and appreciation are due publishers and copyright owners for use of the following.

"Autumn Woods" from A WORLD TO KNOW by James S. Tippett. © 1933 by Harper & Brothers.

"Clipper Ships and Captains" from A BOOK FOR AMERICANS by Rosemary and Stephen Vincent Benet, Holt, Rinehart & Winston, Inc. Copyright, 1933, Rosemary and Stephen Vincent Benet. Copyright renewed © 1961 by Rosemary Carr Benet. Reprinted by permission of Brandt & Brandt Literary Agents, Inc.

"December" from TIRRA LIRRA by Laura E. Richards. Copyright 1932 by Laura E. Richards. Copyright renewed 1960 by Hamilton Richards. Used by permission of Little, Brown & Company.

"Eletelephony" from TIRRA LIRRA by Laura E. Richards. © 1918 by Laura E. Richards. By permission of Little, Brown & Company.

"Far As Man Can See" from THE INDIANS BOOK by Natalie Curtis. Published by Dover Publications. Used by permission.

"Fireworks" by James Reeves. © James Reeves Estate. Reprinted by permission of the James Reeves Estate.

"Hallowe'en Indignation Meeting" from POEMS MADE TO TAKE OUT, © 1963, Margaret Fishback. Published by David McKay Company, Inc.

"In Beauty Happily I Walk" Courtesy American Museum of Natural History.

"In Praise of Water" by Nancy Byrd Turner from CHILD LIFE MAGAZINE, copyright 1929 by Rand McNally & Company.

"Old Father Annum" from THE PETER PATTER BOOK by Leroy F. Jackson. Reprinted by permission of MacMillan Publishing Company.

"Open Range" from COWBOYS AND INDIANS by Kathryn and Byron Jackson. © 1968, 1948 Western Publishing Company, Inc. Used by permission.

"Valentine for Earth" from THE LITTLE NATURALIST by Frances M. Frost. Copyright 1959 by the Estate of Frances M. Frost. Published by Whittlesey House. Used by permission of McGraw-Hill Book Company, Inc.

The editors of Silver Burdett & Ginn Inc. have made every attempt to verify the source of "The Tired Scarecrow," "Mistletoe Gifts," "Great Big House," and "Song of the Crow," but were unable to do so. We believe them to be in public domain.

PICTURE CREDITS

Contributing Artists: Chuck Wimmer 2, 3, 8, 37, 42, 43, 45, 156, 157, 219; Lee Oaskins III 5; Ketti Kupper 10, 168, 169, 171, 178–180, 183; Don Patterson 13, 15, 19; Theresa Fasolino 22, 23; Katherine Ace 25, 49, 101, 129, 149, 165; Steven Schindler 27, 28, 136, 147, 200; Stephen Moscowitz 34; Barbara Lanza 41, 58, 59, 94, 98, 114, 122, 152, 153, 155, 158, 159, 161, 208, 209, 214–217; David Barbara 65; George Baquero 72, 73, 174; Christopher Calle 80, 81, 90; Jeff Cornell 92, 93; Kathy Hendrickson 100, 110, 220, 221; Bill Griffith 105; Jim O'Shea 138; Bill Bell 142, 144, 184, 185, 192–195, 206; Eulala Connor 167; Bill Finewood 168–183; Lee Gaskins 188, 189; Laurie Jordan 218; Nancy Munger 224, 229, 238, 239, 274, Wendy Rasmussen 225, 226, 252; Tom Cardamone 227; Linda Graves 228; Nancy Didion 231; Pat Traub 235, 243, 276, 282, 283; Steve Herfele 242, 259, 263; Susan Melrath 244, 245, 279; David Wisniewski 248; Fred Marvin 250, 251; Jan North 284.

300